How to Raise
the *Next* President

How to Raise
the *Next* President

A Parent's Guide to Giving Your Kid
the Secrets of Success

SALLY SACKS, M.ED., LMHC

Powder Horn Press

To all my wonderful clients,
who have had the courage to help themselves
and to share their lives' challenges with me.
To Jaye, for encouragement and support always.
Thank you. All my love and thanks to
my two beautiful children, Graham and Sydney,
who have taught me most of what I know.
To Chaz, Sarah, and Robert, for gracing our lives
and for teaching me about unconditional love
and courage every day.

Acknowledgements

I would like to thank my parents for being open to learning, even in their later years. I could not ask for better grandparents to my children.

I would like to thank my significant other, Chaz, who parents with me, and who supported my ideas during the writing of this book.

My special thanks go out to Larry at The Floating Gallery for his constant availability, support, and expertise. And thanks to all the editors, artists and production specialists whose skill made this book finally happen.

Contents

Contents

How to Raise
the *Next* President

INTRODUCTION

Sponsoring Emotional Development in Children

"I'm not young enough to know everything."

Zen proverb

I was inspired to write this book by the many children with whom I am in contact every day as a mother and as a professional therapist. I have worked for years with adults who want to know how to be more nurturing, emotionally-aware parents, and how to deal with their own world of feelings and emotions. Inevitably, the work I do with adults to help them become more aware, nurturing parents, takes them back to their own childhood, and the ways in which they were raised.

Unfortunately, many well-meaning parents are often unaware of the job they need to do to help their children develop emotionally. This is because the skills they need were never taught to them. They may know how to intellectually sponsor development; for example, they send children to good schools and enroll them in academic programs to promote success. The children learn how to sing and dance, ski and snowboard, but their positive emotional development is based on their parents' acceptance and appreciation of their own ideas and feelings. Moreover, to ensure such development, parents must give children opportunities to express their own ideas and feelings.

EMOTIONAL DEVELOPMENT

Emotional development in children is their ability to love, to empathize, to forgive, to reason and to value differences — to be open minded, and to find their meaning, purpose, and value in this complex and challenging world. Emotional development means accepting ourselves as we are, imperfect and allowed to make mistakes and move on. In fact, learning how to make mistakes and to deal with imperfection are two of the most important skills you can teach your child. Emotional development is the ability to grow toward maturely managing thoughts, emotions and actions to better your life and others.

Unfortunately, we see the lack of this emotional development in our world today, where hate and self-righteousness, low self-esteem, and lack of acceptance and understanding of others create chaos in our lives. Our reaction to the chaos we live with definitely affects our children. That is why it's so important to know that to promote healthy emotional development in children, we must teach it to them. We must teach them how to think productively versus non-productively, to create a peaceful, happier, more productive life. Many people have no idea how to teach others how to think. This book will show you how. In fact most people think their thinking is natural and not something you create minute-to-minute. I tell my clients to remember that they drive the bus, symbolic of driving their own thoughts and emotions.

Sometimes people don't know how their parents' treatment of them affected their lack of emotional development and thinking, until a major life event, such as loss, death, divorce, or a relationship problem, occurs and causes distress. Then with help, such as psychotherapy, they realize they were taught how to act, be polite, be appropriate, eat all their beans, clean up, wash their hands, and so forth. But they were never asked how they felt or what their ideas were, nor were they sponsored in being comfortable with free expression and thought and making their own decisions.

Lack of emotional development is prevalent in our society. Because of this lack of sponsoring in so many people, we have often valued the workings of the mind over the working of the feelings or emotions. This has caused people to be dissatisfied and unfulfilled in their lives.

I choose to talk about sponsoring emotional awareness or expression of feelings in children, because children usually start out very free-spirited, direct and spontaneous. They express negative and positive feelings with equal skill, without self-judgment until they grow older. At that point, their free spirit can be crushed because of the lack of sponsored emotional development.

If we begin teaching children early on about honoring themselves and their need for free expression, we will help them to be more open, communicative, feeling, and confident adults. How do we teach children to honor themselves? We must honor them.

INSENSITIVITY

I am often concerned as a psychotherapist because many people in my field know their theories and went to excellent schools, but have no idea how to connect with others naturally or deal with their own feelings. Sometimes it seems that intellectual jargon replaces common sense, and often we value that intellectual jargon because of a person's degree or level of schooling. When I meet a psychiatrist, for example, in my field, with more than an intellect, with the additional ability to relate to me or my clients with a heart, I am quite happy. I immediately scoop them up for my practice, because it's important for people treating others with emotional difficulties to be able to connect personally with others. The inability to connect to others in a genuine way is due to lack of knowledge, skill, and opportunity, Harvard degree or not.

We often have leaders in businesses who have lacked emotional sponsoring in growing up and now are in charge of other people. Lack of emotional development produces people who may be harsh, insensitive, unfeeling, and controlling. Possessions and money drive them, and there also is a desire and a need for a sense of power over others. They are overly critical, lack kindness, and are too self-concerned. Many people have problems at work because they are dealing with leaders who have never learned social and emotional skills, such as valuing others, forgiveness, compassion, positive energy, support and reinforcement.

There is barrenness, a lack of soul and depth that comes with lack of emotional awareness. Things become of utmost importance, not people, but as we all travel the road of life, we soon find out that love, connection, and people far surpass the value of material things. The saying that "you can't take it with you when you go" really begins to make sense. You however can take love, forgiveness, empathy and understanding with you when you go.

This book is designed to teach you what sponsoring emotional development in your child means, and what techniques you need to know as a parent to help your child be authentic, open, and comfortable in his/her own skin.

All the intelligence in the world, without emotional awareness, makes life very difficult and a person less than whole. Marriages dissolve or survive. People stay in dead-end jobs because they don't know how to change. Relationships are problematic. Life can feel meaningless and routine, and a large part of interaction is missing, not only with others, but with oneself. If you don't recognize your feelings and act on what they tell you, you cannot be your true free self. It's hard to know your true self, what you value, what your meaning is, and how to feel happy and fulfilled in all areas of your life.

As you read this book, you will understand how you may sponsor or hinder emotional growth in yourself and your children, and hopefully take the steps to live in your emotional world more comfortably, thereby promoting a more comfortable-feeling world for your children. Remember that children live what they see in us as parents.

You have a great gift to offer your children . . . love, love, love, acceptance, and the encouragement to express themselves freely. Teach them how to think effectively, and they'll rule their world, and contribute to the world at large in a more developed way.

ONE

Emotional Awareness in Action

Love Your Monsters

"Mommy," said my then three-year-old son, "If you love your monsters they can't hurt you."

My son blurted out this phrase one day as I picked him up from preschool in the back of my car. As I sat in the driver's seat listening to his words, all my supervisory skills as a trained psychotherapist couldn't compare to what this child summed up in two lines. He had spent many recent nights afraid of the dark, of shadows in the room, and monsters lurking in the closets. Somehow all his fear had culminated in the realization that if you loved these scary monsters, they wouldn't hurt you. If you remain afraid, the monsters will have power.

This is what I spent days, even years, learning myself and teaching adults, and here the natural instinct of a child learned this in a couple of weeks.

I thought about the clients I worked with who had eating disorders or were obese and terrified of eating. Food was their monster, and they wished it would go away. I spent years teaching them to make peace with food because as long as they fought against their urges to eat, food would always maintain power over them. Here my little son understood this concept at age three. I thought about all the monsters we encounter in life: sickness, loss, aging, mental illness, and death, to name a few, and what a gift it would be to understand and embrace these monsters even though they worry us and scare us. He was in preschool, and his thinking was perfect.

THE WISDOM OF CHILDREN

Kids are naturally emotional and spontaneous, and usually open and honest in their feelings. Kids are honest — sometimes, as we know, too honest. They tell us we look old, or tired or chubby, or that we have wrinkles around the eyes. They also tell us that they hate us and love us, need us, want us. They mediate arguments and hug you just when you need it most. They can make you angry as all hell, or you can take one look in their eyes and experience a love like no other.

They also live in their own world, depending on their age, a world that we often as parents don't readily acknowledge or take the time to understand.

Becoming more emotionally aware in our parenting means trying to understand their world and not make theirs be ours. Not only do we want to understand their world, we want to respect it.

For example, when my kids were three and five, I took them to a Marshalls Department store to shop. I needed a break and really wanted time to go shopping. As soon as they got into the store they became wild, completely out of control. They were hiding in empty boxes, playing tag inside the clothes racks, yelling to each other to look at other hiding places. I was embarrassed and angry. These feelings increased as the elderly lady in the corner gave me that look signifying "What a bad parent you are." Other people can often give these looks, which say, "Control these misbehaved kids."

After removing them ashamedly from the store, making sure they hadn't lifted anything, and being ready to take five Valiums, I expressed my feelings angrily. I explained how I just wanted to do one thing for myself, and they wouldn't let me. I continued telling them how I did so much for them and how shamefully they had repaid me. I began thinking of punishments. "Why do you do this," I shouted. "Why?"

My son explained their behavior perfectly. He said that when they see a new place, especially one they've never been to, they need to explore. There are so many corners and crannies and racks to be seen. This was like a giant indoor playground to them, not a store to act well-behaved in. I saw sales on dresses and home furnishings; they saw wide open spaces to be explored. I realized that I had only seen this situation from an adult's point of view and not from the eyes of a child. I realized that I couldn't take them here and expect them to be quiet while I shopped for an hour. They had no interest in the 30%-off sale on bathroom accessories!

Emotional awareness is respecting how children see the world. This wasn't a time to reprimand and punish; it was simply a message to me to pick another time to shop and get some extra help for breaks. This was a hard acceptance for me because having children does cause us to make sacrifices. This is where parents need support, because it's important for it to be okay for us to express our feelings of stress and loss, the loss of being able to do things we did easily before we had children. Many of us, often stemming from how our parents raised us, have "supposed-to's" that don't allow us to see how a child views the world; instead we think in terms of "appropriate behavior." What's appropriate to us is not what seems appropriate to children. Some parents never ask questions or inquire about their child's inner world.

This is not because they are bad parents, but because they are unaware parents.

LISTENING TO YOUR CHILDREN

My daughter and stepdaughter love to play a game of fancy restaurant. My immediate inclination is to stop them, because it requires lots of work. They need good china, help with cooking food, and the undivided attention of us adults. One weekend we promised them they could set it up, and due to our busy schedule we changed our mind, and told them we could do it the next day. We then made a plan, not considering what they had planned for the restaurant. They started crying, and told us that we didn't believe that they could create a real restaurant. They said they had worked really hard the day before to set things up, and plan the meal, and we weren't taking them seriously. They had wanted to do something kind for us by having us dine in their café.

We decided that they needed to do this, and that we had ignored their needs. We set them free to do their thing. When they called us down to eat at BERNANETT'S, the name they had picked, we found an unbelievable scene. There was candlelight, music, lace table cloths, candles and they had rearranged all the pictures neatly on the walls. My daughter was the waitress, and my stepdaughter was the chef, and the food and presentation were magnificent. Truly we had underestimated their abilities, and minimized how important this was to them. We praised them, thanked them, and really enjoyed ourselves. We apologized for not thinking about how important this was to them. They accepted our apology, and once a month we now eat at BERNANETT'S.

I stumbled across my son's idea of why he acted the way he did in a store because he offered me the information. Something made me open to listening, and listening is the key. The same need to listen applied to my girls. I had to look and listen to see how important that restaurant was to them. It wasn't just a kid's game. Listen to your children.

PARENTAL EXPECTATIONS

Many parents have expectations, that kids should act well-behaved in a store, and not dirty the kitchen or use kitchen dishware. These are examples where you have to use emotional intelligence to decide what's more important, squelching a child's emotional development or being polite and orderly. Even if you need to remove your young children from a store because they're exploring too much, do it for the right reasons. If the reason is to take them home to play because it's too hard to sit still in the store, take them home. But don't take them home telling them they're misbehaving when they are being kids.

For example, many parents want to go to a restaurant, even with their two-year-old. This sounds reasonable, right? Getting out is necessary! Yet the parent may also want the two-, three-, or four-year-old to be extremely quiet and well- behaved. Most kids this age do not go to a restaurant to be well-behaved. They have energy. They want to run, see things, explore, and even play with their food. Some parents become stressed to the max because their child won't sit quietly. They'll even describe seeing another family with a perfectly quiet kid. Well, maybe that child is naturally, inherently quieter, but maybe he or she is forced to be that way due to restrictive, controlling rules. These kinds of rules put on young children can be very destructive. These kids may grow into overly conforming adults, or become rebellious.

We can begin teaching polite behavior in a restaurant at a young age, but with realistic expectations. Again, find babysitting to have a quiet, non-stressed dinner if you have young children.

If we lack some acceptance of children's needs for self-expression and to have a world apart from us, we might look at our own upbringing and parenting. If we place a lot of "shoulds" on our child, they probably apply to how we were raised. If we are too rigid, it probably was how we were parented; we may be copying our parents. Remember children learn by what they see more than by what they're told.

Gaining insight into ourselves is valuable because it

helps us become more emotionally aware of our own upbringing and how we may be affecting our children due to that upbringing.

UNEVEN DEVELOPMENT

If we haven't valued or listened to our feelings, it will be difficult to listen to our children's.

Many educated parents may not know how to express their feelings, ask their kids questions, look into their eyes and ask about their day. For many they don't even see how their lack of emotional awareness affects their children. Usually, others notice the problem, or years later the child, now adult, comes to therapy. They usually come because they find themselves unhappy and unfulfilled, dealing with troublesome emotions like anger, anxiety, and depression, and/or with problematic relationships. Many problems like depression and anxiety have a biological component, but are also associated with years of the lack of free expression, and years of reinforcing negative, non-productive thinking.

There are many adults that have uneven social development because their emotional needs went unaddressed while their intellectual needs were fostered and encouraged. The Massachusetts Institute of Technology even noticed this and developed "Charm School," designed to help students develop more social skills and connect to others more easily around a table setting. There were so many kids whose parents put an importance on intellect that they forgot to help their child develop social skills. A life is very difficult, and opportunities are hindered if one can't as much as make small talk with another. This is how we connect to others and make friends

When we parent with conscious emotional awareness, being mindful in what we do, we think about our behavior, and our children's behavior. We consciously assess why they might be doing something, and why we are responding in a certain way. We assess ourselves, our beliefs and behaviors, and are open minded to trying different approaches if we see one doesn't work. This is emotional awareness, sensing what your child needs, and how she/he is feeling, respecting those feelings, also being aware of our own needs and the situation at hand. We listen, we openly express feelings and encourage it in our kids, and we show understanding. We are aware of the skills and conditions children need to grow emotionally.

THINKING OF OTHERS

Once while in Harvard Square with my son, we passed a homeless man looking desperate and sick. He was asking for money and thanking people going by whether they gave or not. Recognizing this man's behavior is emotional awareness. My son passed him and as we walked he asked me to wait a minute. He went back on his own at age five to give the man some coins he had brought to the square. He came back saying only that the man looked hungry. This was the perfect opportunity for me to sponsor this behavior and show of feeling in him, and I did. I watched many adults carry on with their day, very few stopping to notice the man. Children are aware. They notice situations and live in the moment. This ability is already advanced emotional intelligence. Most of us adults spend years trying to meditate to stay in the moment, while children do this naturally.

My daughter, at age five, was shopping with me for school clothes. Every time she passed a pretty outfit in a smaller size, she wanted to buy it for a two-year-old friend named Julia. Thinking of others is part of her nature, and again I reinforce that behavior in her. I make sure it doesn't go unnoticed. Catch the behavior, and re-inforce it. I would say to her, "You are such a kind person to think of Julia. That's why I'm so lucky to have you for my daughter." I follow this with a big hug.

I was watching two nine-year-old boys on the play-ground tease another boy because he was smaller and not as skilled at doing wheelies on his bike. They were laughing at him, and you could see the younger boy was hurt. Another child, a nine-year-old, came to the boy's aid and in their language, acting very cool, said, "Hey guys, lay off, enough." They got it and stopped because they respected their friend. Friends and their opinions are very important to children. Children are emotionally aware and can show empathy for others. The child protecting his friend has learned to do that somewhere from example. This is behavior we don't want to miss encouraging and rewarding. Children who go with the crowd, or who are afraid to ask questions and express their own feelings, have often not had positive examples of free self-expression.

If we are aware of children's natural ability to think, feel, and even maintain order, as in the above situation, then we have to use less control and provide more sponsoring of what they already possess, the ability to know how they feel and how others feel. We will create independent thinkers.

Again, often due to our parental lack of awareness of our abilities as children, we may be missing these chances to listen to kids and appreciate the wisdom they offer. We may be too quick to control and manage their affairs. We may overrule their independent ideas, not recognizing their importance. We may miss opportunities to respect and value their intuitive nature.

I believe that a parent's job is to teach, provide for, and protect their children, while listening to their ideas and feelings and valuing them. The parent's job isn't to control their child, imposing their values and ideas on the child with little regard for the child's needs and wants.

HARRY

I was speaking to a woman whose son, Harry, had pierced his ear at age nine. He had felt lonely and unpopular in school and wasn't telling anyone how he felt. He saw a kid's show where the popular boy had a pierced ear and became the coolest kid in school, and felt if he had one it could make him popular, too. So he pierced his ear alone in a dangerous, unsanitary way and put in an earring.

When mom found out she was faced with a dilemma. First, his feelings were important. He, as a nine-year-old came up with an idea to make himself popular. An adult has ideas like this too. "Maybe if I dye my hair, or get a breast augmentation, I'll be more attractive." Because he's a kid, he didn't know how to do it safely and did something that angered his mother because he could have really hurt himself. So the mom is faced with helping him deal with his feelings of being unpopular, as well as teaching him how to do things safely. Punishing this child would only make him feel worse, and devalue both his feelings and the solution to his problem. His desire to help himself and improve his self-image has to be appreciated as well.

Parents do punish their kids for doing things like this because they are looking at an act of disobedience to them, rather than the emotional world of the child. If you don't deal with the child's emotional world, they will not learn how to experience and cope with their feelings. The emotions of this child are telling you that he felt uncomfortable enough with himself that he felt he had to do something to change himself. The parent has to recognize his feelings and give him the opportunity to talk about them. If the parent were raised with their own feelings going unaddressed, they may not address their child's feelings because they don't even recognize a problem.

Fortunately, this mom was sensitive to her boy's needs, and although she was empathetic toward his attempt to be more popular, she also explained the ramifications of doing something like this without proper equipment, and her anger and concern about those elements of his action. On the other hand, she encouraged him to talk to her next time, that she was there for him when he was feeling badly about himself in school or anywhere.

In the case above, I would encourage the parent to tell the child a story about when they were young and had similar feelings. Children love stories and feel safe when they know that others have felt insecure, scared, and unsure, too.

CAROLINE

Caroline was a seventeen-year-old in high school. Her mother did not want her to get a tattoo, but despite her mother's disapproval, she got one. Her mom was furious and felt that this was an attack on her. Mom had told her daughter how she felt about tattoos, and daughter deliberately disobeyed her. The two fought over this, both feeling hurt. Now the tattoo is permanent. Was there any benefit to yelling at and condemning the child? No. The mother, one hopes, when the child expressed a desire for a tattoo, brought up the dangers and the need for an experienced artist who uses clean needles. This would have been very important for the mother to do even if she said "No tattoos," because the reality is that the girl is grown and may still get one. Remember that the daughter's idea of what's good to do is different from her parents', and if you're a seventeen-year-old, it's your body; if you have a safe way to get a tattoo, you may do it. So the parent has to pick her battles and be prepared. Kids live in their own world, with their own ideas.

The mom would have done better to express her feelings openly, especially her dismay that her daughter got a tattoo; at the same time, she might find something positive or humorous to say, and might let her know what it takes to remove a tattoo, should she decide to get another one. In time, the girl may realize on her own —

for example, when she wants it removed — that the mom was right. But let her learn on her own. Remember this saying: "Do you want to be right, or do you want to get along?" Respect and keep an open mind.

Even a child who gets a tattoo against his or her parents' wishes is showing independent thinking. We may not like this in a hard-to-manage high-schooler, but the value of independent thinking in the long term is a good thing. If we recognize this, we can still be upset at our child's action, while still appreciating their thought process. It is important to also note that there are some kids who wouldn't get the tattoo because they know their parents would be upset. It would be a good thing if these kids do what they do out of respect and consideration for their parents. It is good if parents can create an atmosphere of mutual respect, rather than get the desired behavior out of control, with no humor. Example: "Tattoos look trashy and cheap, so don't you dare get one."

POLITENESS VS. GENUINE SELF-EXPRESSION

I was at a children's party one holiday with friends. There were lots of treats and presents, and one mom kept insisting her child say thank you for every single piece of food, trinket, etc. She'd walk over each time to her child and say, "Did you say thank you for that?" over and over without giving any attention to the fact the child had already said it ten times. Finally, the child looked at her and said, "Yes!" emphatically. The child was saying, "Stop managing me and let me be!"

Do we confuse commanding politeness and being nice to others with fostering self-appreciation and acceptance? If you're polite to people because your parents have ordered you to be polite, it's a rule, not a real form of self-expression. If you've laid down all these rules on your children with a lack of emotional awareness in parenting, then the politeness is simply a false mask that the child wears to do the right thing and to be approved by parents and others. Politeness becomes the child's mask put on in order to be liked, rather than the child's feeling accepted and liked inside; therefore, the child naturally treats others the same way. I call this the Eddie Haskell syndrome. Eddie was a TV character in the 60's who tried so hard to be polite to his friends' parents that he nauseated them and everyone else around.

Our goal as parents is to sponsor the natural expressions of the feelings that we would like to see in our children — again by example.

Teaching Kindness

If you want your child to be kind, don't order them to be kind. Consciously show them examples of kindness by doing things with them that are kind to others and letting them hear you talk about how kind someone was and how good that felt to you. Send a card to a sick friend, take advantage of the school charity drive, or give canned goods to a local shelter. Have them pack nice clothes they can't wear anymore to give to children in need. Make sure you allow them to save clothes that may be special to them — even if you want to get rid of them! Compliment others who are kind and bring it to their awareness without comparing or being judgmental toward them. Show them daily appreciation of people, places and things in your and their lives.

If I want to teach my children a lesson in kindness, I'll consciously say, "Did you hear what people are doing for that little boy who is sick?" They'll ask what, and I'll tell them some nice thing the community did and comment, "Isn't that great!" enthusiastically. They learn it's a respectful and admirable thing to be kind and thoughtful to others and you will reinforce that behavior in them.

If you want your children to express what they are feeling, give them that opportunity by expressing your own feelings honestly and directly, and by giving them room to express themselves, unlike the woman forcing and managing her daughter's thanks. Reminding a child how it feels to be thanked is a good thing. Forcing them by controlling and managing is not. Ask them questions, express happiness, anger, concerns, joy, and so on.

Expressing Your Feelings

One great forum in which to express feelings and teach your children to be open and honest with you is the family meeting. It's good to hold one each week, at the same time each week if possible for continuity and structure. Kids usually love them and look forward to them.

For example, one night I was feeling very upset that no one ever helped me to clean up after dinner. I had cleaned up alone time and time again, doing it quickly to get it over with so I could take a break. I was feeling very angry and resentful, like a fishwife in my home, taken for granted. I decided to call a family meeting to express my feelings so I'd be less resentful and get some help that I felt I deserved. I told my family that I felt angry and resentful and that I felt I had to let these feelings out. The kids listened and understood, as did my husband. The kids agreed that they would pick up their dishes, and my husband and I would take turns clearing the other dinner foods. I felt great that I had let things out, and felt that I had taught them to do the same.

They were able to empathize about how their behavior was affecting me. I told them I was feeling frustrated and angry. This allowed them to see and understand these feelings, and to know that it's OK to tell someone you have these feelings, rather than hold them in.

In fact, the next day, my daughter told me that she was feeling frustrated that I wasn't listening to her, and I know she learned to express that by listening to me. I was very pleased.

Another time, my son was invited to a friend's house and the friend asked my daughter if she'd like to come too, because a couple of girls she didn't know but were her age would be there. I asked my daughter if she'd like to go, and she said, "I don't feel comfortable with that today, since I don't know the girls well." She was very assertive in her statement, and I was very proud that I had given her the language, through example, of how to go with her feelings. Using words that express your feelings gives the child the ability to know how to express them: "I don't feel comfortable in that dress." "I'd like to go, but I really need to get some sleep and relax." "I love to go out and talk with my friends." "Good friends are wonderful, aren't they?" "I'm so glad you're my daughter/son." "It's so fun to hang out with you, you're a really kind person."

REINFORCING KIND BEHAVIOR

Using positive reinforcement words for their emotional behavior makes children feel good about themselves. "You were so thoughtful and kind, holding the elevator for that older person. I'm so glad that you are my son." As well as in everyday life, family meetings are a good place to compliment your children on their behavior and thinking.

Use kind, expressive words as often as you can with your children and with yourself.

A little friend Nina came back from a trip to Europe with her parents. She went to Italy for three weeks. In detail, she described their accommodations, the people, and the food, and when she was finished she said to my kids and me, "You know, before I went to Europe, you know, you live in Acton, and you only think there is Acton. And your world is only here. And then you go to Europe and you see how big it is, and how much there is to see." We all had a discussion about what was different and where we'd like to visit. These are the emotional opportunities we can't afford to overlook. This little girl was expressing her emotional insight and feeling that the world was this big incredible place, bigger than she ever knew. This kind of thinking and feeling needs much praise, recognition and reinforcement.

Children will listen to themselves if we make that

possible by respecting them as individuals with rights to their own ideas and beliefs. Encourage them to make decisions and state their opinions. Reward them for their insight and spontaneous thoughts, actions, and observations.

In the following chapter we will look at examples of how the sponsoring, or lack of sponsoring of emotional development in parenting, affects our children.

Two

Cases to Learn From

JENNA AND HARRIET

Jenna, age five, and her mom Harriet, came to counseling because Mom was concerned about Jenna's angry attitude and hitting. Jenna apparently got so mad at her mom that she would hit her and tell her she hated her, and Harriet was concerned Jenna had an "anger management problem." She actually called me describing her daughter's problem as just that, an "anger management problem." I already assessed that Mom was a "thinker" and not a "feeler." Words like "appropriate," and "behavior management problem" *per se*, if you will, are often indicators that someone is in their intellectual world and not in their emotional one. The words are formal and global, not personal.

To Harriet, hitting was unacceptable. I asked her when her daughter would hit her, and she said it was often when she didn't get her immediate needs met, and when Harriet was giving attention to Jenna's older sister. "She always has to be the center of attention," said Harriet. "I don't know where she learned that. She's so selfish."

I asked her what she did when Jenna hit her and Harriet said she'd get angry at Jenna and send her to her room for hitting because hitting was wrong and bad.

Harriet didn't talk to her or ask her why she was hitting her and talk about how it hurt her. All she knew is that hitting is bad, and what if she hits others. Harriet also felt Jenna's anger was over-reactive and didn't want to sponsor it. "She's very dramatic," Harriet would say in front of her, not realizing how this critical remark, which ignored Jenna's feelings, was affecting her. I had already assessed that someone had devalued Harriet's own feelings.

Here, Harriet has missed finding out any emotional clues as to why her child is angry. Therefore, Harriet is angry and the child's feelings go unaddressed. The mother has already decided what the feelings are: selfishness and neediness. When a person labels your feelings without asking you what they are, it doesn't encourage you to be open and expressive with them. It also causes a great deal of anger that can go on for years and affect healthy self-esteem.

What Harriet came to realize in counseling was that she never allowed herself to behave, think, or act freely, and this did make her angry toward others who gave themselves freedom of expression. She had all these restrictive rules in her head coming from her own childhood, and she was repeating the same lack of emotional awareness in parenting her daughter. No one had ever asked her how she felt in her family; she just did what she was told at the expense of her own free self-expression. Her daughter's free self-expression made her angry and jealous, and she made sure she stopped it, just as it was stopped in her. She realized that she didn't keep the hitting "relational" between mother and daughter, acknowledging feelings and talking to her, but went "global," saying that hitting was wrong and inappropriate. Her rule that her daughter must go to her room when her daughter hit her became a rule with no feelings attached. The child had no way to work out her anger or to understand that anger was justifiable at times. The child needs to learn how to accept her feelings and manage them. If these feelings go unaddressed, she can't manage them.

Emotional awareness may have Harriet going into her daughter's room, talking to her about her anger, and supporting her, while letting her know that it hurts to be hit and that hitting isn't OK. Children do need teaching and guidance. The child's anger needs to be acknowledged and she needs to be taught better coping skills to deal with it, just like adults. Mom might have to look at her own behavior and make some changes; perhaps the child's anger is justified. Mom's understanding and apology will most likely make her child very happy.

JACKIE

Now, let's look at Jackie. She was at the dinner table with her parents, who had prepared a special meal for some visitors. When it came time for the lasagna with broccoli and an interesting cheese sauce, Jackie, age eight, said she didn't like the cheese sauce and just wanted plain broccoli. Her parents were upset and informed her that she should "just try it, it's too hard to get the cheese sauce off." They reprimanded her for not trying it, and labeled her a picky eater and difficult in front of the guests: "Mark eats anything, but not Jackie!"

A parent informed by emotional awareness would ask, "Does the child have a right to dislike a meal?" What about including children in the discussion of what they would like for dinner, especially if they're eating at the party? Most of us would ask an adult whether they liked or disliked a certain food, so why not do so with a child? Certainly, if we didn't ask, we wouldn't embarrass them because they didn't like lasagna. Kids do have a right to make choices, and their bodies often tell them what kind of food they want. As we all know as parents, their tastes are often different than ours. Kids' taste is sometimes so different, it seems as though they come from the planet Fructose. Sometimes we have to listen to our kids and affirm their right to their own tastes, or else we develop a child who can't listen to their own needs, emotionally and physically. It's good to allow children choices. It helps them to be assertive and decide for themselves in areas where they can.

Again, we have to assess as parents why we are making this rule — that our children have to eat foods they dislike. Is it politeness? Is it fear of your kids looking bad in front of guests? Is it a desire for your child to try something different? In the case of Jackie's parents, it was a little of everything mentioned. They wanted their child to be polite at the expense of her own feelings, because this was done to them when they were children. But they also felt their child was a picky eater and not open to food diversity. That may be true, but in this forum, in this forceful and critical way, you can't get the child to try something new. The parent would be better off trying to get their child to try a new food at a better time, without outside people. The parents for example could introduce broccoli, and encourage the child through positive language to try it. You could say, "This stuff makes you strong. Try it." If the child gives it a try, fantastic. Easy. If the child resists insistently, explain why it's important to eat vegetables, etc., and try again soon. Forcing never works. Patience does.

Including children in discussions about their lunch, about meals, and about what they'd like to wear allows them to express themselves and to become independent thinkers. If you allow a child to listen to what his/her body likes to eat, and when he/she likes to eat, the child will follow inner cues of hunger, and not eat according to the clock or because he/she sees another person eating. Many adults with weight problems never learned to follow their inner cues about hunger. There were too many rules around eating, too many restrictions.

Affirming Kids' Choices

I once knew a mom who insisted that all the expensive sneakers the kids were buying were ridiculous. Her seven-year-old boy wore baby-style hand-me-downs while the group in his neighborhood all wore the ones in style. The woman, based on her principles, refused to buy her son the sneakers even though he wanted them and felt left out. Again, emotional awareness is needed here. We can't confuse our values with our kids' when they are old enough to make some decisions. This woman could afford the sneakers, another story that also requires emotional awareness. Her not buying them made the child feel different without any explanation other than that she thought the sneakers were ridiculous. That meant his friends were ridiculous, and his feelings were also ridiculous. It might be more helpful to try to get the child the sneakers; maybe he can use his allowance or birthday money if you feel they're too expensive. Maybe the sneakers can be a Hanukkah or Christmas gift. But helping him to figure out a way that works for both of you is fair. In this child's case, he was left out of many things because he wasn't allowed to try to be in with the crowd. Again, this can be controlling behavior on the part of the parent, not sponsoring and being emotionally aware. Later in life this child may feel guilty giving himself nice things or he may feel superior criticizing others for wanting unnecessary trivia in their lives. On introspection, his mother might find that she had someone tell her the same things that she was telling her son.

For example, how many parents love certain movies, and games that their children like. Many parents have taken children to a movie because the kids are excited about it. If the movie is safe, and age appropriate, we might have to make that sacrifice for the child, and pray that we can find some enjoyment out of it! We don't have to love something, be it a movie, a game, a toy, to sponsor it or respect our kids' liking for it. We may think it's stupid or silly or a waste of time, but what if our child likes it? Do we forbid it in the house? Do we insult what they like, and call it stupid? If we think something is very detrimental we may forbid it, but even that deserves an explanation why, and you must judge whether you are being fair or making your needs your child's.

I was at the store in a long line with my daughter. She wanted a gumball as big as her head, and I said no, explaining why. It was too big, too bad for her teeth, and would spoil her appetite before supper. Moreover, I didn't want her to choke. The lady behind the register told her that her teeth would fall out if she ate that thing. While waiting in line, my daughter said assertively, "I don't care, it's more money from the Tooth Fairy."

"Now that's a smart kid" said a man behind me. Leave it to kids to know it all, and once again to live in their own world apart from us adults.

As parents, we need to respect the spontaneous intuitive nature of our children. We need to sponsor it, not squelch it.

In my gumball example, we may say no to our child because the big gumball is sugary and bad for the teeth. We explain to them our reason for not wanting them to have it, but we give them credit for their independent thinking.

Rules, Right and Wrong

I once worked with a woman whose son wanted a tape by a rap artist who used very derisive words against women. His mother didn't want him to listen to it, but also was emotionally aware enough to know that he might listen to it on the radio or at another child's house. When her son asked her to help him buy the tape, she was in a situation to teach him something. As a woman she found it very offensive, and didn't want to support her son listening to the singer. But she emphasized that she couldn't support her son's desire for the tape due to the way it made her feel. She assertively stated her feelings. This taught her son something and was a much more productive technique than calling his desire for the tape, or the rapper stupid or bad. The lyrics may be annoying and obnoxious, but there are more productive vs. less productive means of getting this message across to a teen. It's not about being right, it's about techniques that get your point across versus techniques that are ineffective.

In kindergarten, my son went to his gym class and wanted to play basketball after seeing balls all around. My son had played basketball since he was three at the YMCA, was very athletic and coordinated, and was rewarded and treated with respect by his family and friends for his athletic prowess and good sportsmanship. My son came home upset this gym day saying the gym teacher told him that he was too young to play basketball and that they did not allow games, ("It's too competitive"). I, being keen on emotional development and concerned about the message my son was given, talked with the gym teacher on my next visit to the school. He confirmed that he had said this, and I explained to him how this affected my child. First of all, it denied any ability he had, lumped kids by age into one group, and contradicted what he'd been doing well and freely for two years. It disregarded him as an individual in favor of an arbitrary rule based on non-competitiveness. This is unfair, and he understood this. These things happen all the time, and it's helpful as parents to become aware of them and to educate others.

One little girl was at her preschool and during clean-up a teacher found her pulling her chair out of the class-room into a quiet place in the hall. "What are you doing?" asked the teacher. "I don't want to clean up," she said, "so I'm taking a time out." The time out was an arbitrary rule, with no understanding conveyed around it.

If a rule is a rule, the child will work around it and not understand that cleaning up helps others.

THE KINDNESS OF CHILDREN

I once worked with a client who was in a very bad marriage; it had deteriorated rapidly and a great deal of anger and hate was being expressed. He had a three-year-old son, and one day after a heated, hateful argument, his little son found him near tears in the den. The child handed him a Kleenex and hugged him. Unfortunately, this man needed a lot of work to become mature enough emotionally to see how his and his wife's behavior was affecting his boy.

Kids are smart; they know the scoop. The little boy mentioned was aware of his dad's pain and gave him what he needed. He was young enough to know everything.

In Dunkin' Donuts, I watched a young man in line help a little child trying to get by another adult in line to get to his mom on the other side. The adult didn't see the child stuck in front of him, so the young man reached for the child to help her out, making the other man aware she was there and stuck. My son and daughter were very impressed by this customer's kindness and helping way. I enforced their observations by saying how most people are kind, including them. Next they started bragging about how they did a kind thing! "Remember when, oh yeah, well remember when I . . ." It was great. Kids sense when there is emotional intelligence and when there's a lack of it. We can see this when kids don't like a teacher or a babysitter, and we as adults know why.

It's important to listen to who they like and dislike too, and ask them why.

Sometimes we ignore this as parents. For example a child may say, "Mrs. Simms embarrassed me today in class," and the parent might say, "Well, what did you do?" before identifying with how bad that might have felt, and asking what happened. It would be more productive to say, "That must have felt bad to be embarrassed. What happened? Tell me." This makes the child feel heard, and allows you to teach the child something when you get the information.

Kids like kind, emotive people. They are intuitive, and we must listen to them, learn from them, and value their thoughts and opinions. Kids like people who respect them and are open and direct with them. Just try asking them about who they want to stay with when you're away. Kids will show love and feeling to those whom they know show it toward them. They also know who is capable of taking care of them, and who isn't. I once had a very funny client come to me years ago. I asked about her family history, and she said this to me. "Let me sum it up for you. When I was old enough to comprehend things, about three or four years old, I took one look at the two people in charge of raising me, and said, oops, am I in trouble. I don't think that they have a clue."

BLAMING THE CHILD

I once worked with a pre-teen who had been in all kinds of trouble in school. Her single dad was concerned and, due to a friend's suggestion, brought her in for counseling. He said that she hung out with a tough crowd, stayed out too late, and never told the truth about her whereabouts. He blamed her, saying that she had little accountability for her behavior.

When I spoke with the client about her dad's concerns, she was amazed at his concern considering "his immature behavior." She reported that he often stayed out later than he had said, usually drinking at a local bar. She said he'd never apologize when he got home, and often he left her alone for a long time. She recognized his difficulty in relating to her emotionally, too. Dad had trouble being a parent, and his daughter was well aware of this. Not unless Dad got help for himself emotionally could he help his daughter. His daughter was angry that she was being scapegoated as the problem.

USING HUMOR

I remember when I was a housemother to teenagers years ago, and I took them to an area where all their friends hung out. They were teenage girls and saw some boys they liked. I was their counselor and housemother, so when they saw the boys they asked me to duck down in the car so they would not look un-cool with the house counselor. Well, this was an odd request since I was the driver, and I did let them know that I couldn't duck down and safely get us home! But I also assured them that I wouldn't embarrass them either. I won't even talk, I joked! I was saying to them that I understood their need to be cool, and my self-esteem could handle them not wanting me to appear and embarrass them. In my mind I was cool and that's all that mattered! If you are a parent and wouldn't duck down in such a situation, let the teenagers know you understand their feelings, but you're their parent and are not hiding. They'll see you respecting yourself, even though you're understanding them. Many things children do relate to how they view the world at their age. It's not about us. Again, we need to acknowledge and respect their independent world.

I use the example of my experience as a counselor because I think many parents take their children's reactions to them too much to heart, without being aware that these kids live in a different world and will change with age, just as most of us adults have. Sometimes it is hard to wait for that change. Sometimes it's really hard, and we as parents need support. While we're waiting for that change, we can accept them, and, in the above case with the teenagers, use words like, "Gee, I thought I was pretty cool!" or "OK, I'll make the drop quickly so you won't be embarrassed by your loving, caring mom!" Use humor, and be open. Humor is such a great tool in working with kids, because it lightens up situations and allows you to connect emotionally.

EMOTIONAL GROWTH FOR PARENTS

Being able to respect ourselves and our kids means working on our own personal growth as parents and people as our children work on theirs. Remember our own self-expression, maturity level, confidence, emotional awareness and ideas all serve to guide our parenting, so it's important for us as parents to grow and to examine ourselves and our behavior. It's important for us as parents to sometimes lighten up and pick our battles, to be more accepting, humorous and relaxed. These are skills that we as parents may have never learned in our own families of origin. We can see the challenge sponsoring emotional awareness in our children presents. You have to learn it to give it!

When we grow emotionally we have more awareness,

humor, flexibility open-mindedness, and patience. We communicate more freely and become less trapped in our feelings and emotions. We learn how to talk from our own point of view, expressing ourselves openly and directly, and encouraging that in our kids. For example you might say: "When you come home late and I don't know where you are, I worry terribly because I love you and I don't know what happened to you. I'm left up in the air. This is why I want you to call. I'm your parent and since it's still my job to take care of you, I need to know where you are. I always let Dad know where I am so he doesn't worry. Please call me when you're late so I know where you are. Thank you."

This is a lot different than saying "You need to call me" in a controlling tone, showing control and lack of trust. The child will pick up on your belief in him and act accordingly.

Reasoning and Openness

Expressing why you require certain behavior lets a child know what the rules are about, and even if they don't always follow them, you've laid a foundation for understanding and reasoning. This will help your child to communicate effectively in his or her relationships.

It is important to remember that children usually do as

we do, not as we say. If you check in about your whereabouts, do kind things for others, and work toward self-confidence and personal growth in yourself, your child will mirror these behaviors.

As you grow, so does your child.

Emotional awareness means direct communication. You need to look at where your kids are in their development and state your feelings and needs without issuing control or allowing yourself to feel extreme guilt, or extreme anger. Remember, direct and honest expression in you sponsors the same in your children. Sometimes, as parents, we have to lose it, to remind ourselves that we need to gain control over our own emotions.

Again, reasoning teaches them volumes more than orders and demands. For example, when my children need to go to bed, and don't want to, it is annoying to me that they are keeping me up. What I have learned works with them is to say, "Guys, I really need your cooperation. I am really tired and can't go to bed and shut down the house if you refuse to go to bed. Please help me out and get in bed, so we can all get some sleep."

If you control and don't respect, value, or listen, you'll create children that don't fully express their own opinions or know what they want. They will make decisions based on "shoulds," not feelings. Externals will always guide their decisions, not internal cues.

If you are too lenient, and sponsor or support all of

your children's needs and not your own, your children will rule and you will end up resentful and stressed. Your children will also pick up on you as being a person without needs, and lose respect for you or become a person without needs themselves. If you show you have needs too, you will gain respect.

Direct, honest, and open communications of feelings is the way to go, and for people who have trouble with this, get assistance — it really helps. Counseling can really help people to express themselves openly, provided you choose a helping person with emotional intelligence.

I am reminded often of a common-sense parenting story which happened about ten years ago at a friend's baby shower on Cape Cod. A bunch of moms with teens were talking about their problems, mostly with times and curfews; the kids came home late often and the moms would punish them. One woman, a quiet, very connecting type of person, was asked if she had ever had this problem. She stated that she hadn't, because when her seventeen-year-old boy was young (five years old), the family had had a meeting and had made a pact that they always would let each other know where they were, for family reasons, safety, if they were leaving on a trip, and so forth. So, for her son, calling in was as regular as brushing his teeth. It wasn't about control at all. The reasons were caring, family responsibility, and consideration. The parents always left their son all the numbers where they could be reached, no matter where they went. There was no rule based on mistrust or fear that mandated that the family members call; this was simply done for everybody's well-being. There was a respect for one another, and desire for cooperation out of that respect.

To express your needs and feelings to your child and let them express theirs to you openly gives them the gift of internal freedom. And a valuable gift this is indeed.

In the following chapter, we will take a look at what happens when you become more emotionally aware of your needs and your children's, and you find yourself in situations with others who have not been so enlightened. You can run into trouble unless you learn to protect yourself.

Three

Different Strokes

One thing that becomes difficult when you gain awareness about how to be more emotionally intelligent is dealing with families and other parents, people who may be your friends, who aren't as emotionally aware. In fact, when you become more emotionally in tune you are aware, not only in parenting, but in many other life situations, of the lack of emotional development in business, schools and individuals.

DEALING WITH DIFFERING PARENTING STYLES

For example, John was an active five-year-old boy who was over at the house of his friend Carl. Carl was quiet by nature, but was also not allowed to run or have much freedom in his home. John's mom had a designated place in her house where kids could run and play freely, so when John went to Carl's he would run. Carl's parents, by their looks, made it very clear to John's parents that running wild was not good behavior, and they were parents who put a lot of emphasis on being well-behaved and calm. Every time John's parents left Carl's parents' house, they would feel bad, especially John's mother. She began to resent her friend and didn't like this because they had been friends for a long time, despite their personality differences. Sometimes John would really get too energetic and not listen, and that was easy to handle. Mom would talk to him when they left, or have him apologize, explaining that different folks have different rules, and when you're in someone else's house, even if they're different from your own, you need to respect their rules. Her child understood this. Her concern was not wanting to visit her friend because she was so conscious of the friend watching her child to make sure he wasn't too wild or rough. This wasn't comfortable for John's mom, because she began to feel uncomfortable when around the family, fearing her child would be reprimanded unfairly. John wasn't an overly aggressive, rough child. He just had a more energetic, physical component than her friend's child and this was not bad. This was a difference to be understood and respected.

Because John was so frequently reprimanded by these parents when around their boy, his mom found it necessary to be open with him about what was happening. She told him Carl's family didn't wrestle and play sports a lot and they didn't understand that it's fun for other kids. They are more afraid than we are that their son will get hit by a ball, or clothes will get dirty, or that he will get hurt. We think differently. Her son, because she had always been so open with him, understood this very well. He was even able to accept his friend and their differences.

John's mom saw Carl's mom as lacking emotional intelligence about boys and play. Carl's mom herself was raised very strictly and was rather rigid and proper. She was a kind woman, but without a lot of play or humor about herself or the world. She labeled things appropriate and inappropriate according to her view of the world. Be careful of words like appropriate and inappropriate. They are often judgmental and rigid labels. In some cases, they do apply but many less emotionally-aware parents use the terms too regularly.

Emotional intelligence also means accepting your friends as they are and working with them unless they are acquaintances and you don't mind the loss of the friendship. But friends who differ and would like to remain friends need to talk, to learn from each other, and to be honest with feelings. Hopefully, it will be possible for them to resolve their differences. In most lasting friendships, people do. Parents need to communicate their feelings to other parents, too.

Some parents won't believe in boys or girls playing with a violent toy, *e.g.*, a sword, or they might not let their kids watch movies that you feel are harmless. As a parent, you will run into these differences constantly. There may be children who have never seen a McDonald's or Burger King and others who live there. But all you can do is to choose friends you feel comfortable with most of the time and talk with others, or to understand that in other houses there are different sets of rules and see if you and your child feel comfortable. The emotionally-aware parent who teaches her child to be emotionally aware will understand about different parenting styles and explain why watching Disney is not allowed at Mary's house. If a parent likes Disney, he/she can say, "We don't feel the same way Mary's parents feel, but we can respect their rule in their house." You need to make sure as a parent that the rules are fair. When someone makes you or your child feel bad because you are doing something they find inappropriate, like letting your child play with a sword, or watching a movie you feel is okay, then again you need to talk to that person or end your relations with him or her — again depending on your and your child's respective levels of discomfort.

Parenting Styles and Self-Awareness

However, I think people make unwarranted assumptions when they lack emotional awareness. For example, in one neighborhood where a client of mine lived, a group of parents forbade their boys to have toy guns. This seemed like a good idea. But my client allowed her three-year-old to play with toy guns because she felt he'd make one anyway, just as other kids made guns out of toilet paper rolls, sticks, vacuum cleaner parts, and so forth. Saying "no" was related to the grown-ups' fear of guns; the child could actually play with the toy gun and know that real guns aren't good because they kill people. Toy guns don't. Kids get this; they are not stupid. This particular mom felt that not letting her child have the toy gun could cause more problems. Many parents underestimate their child's ability to know right from wrong. Again, the goal is to live with and talk about differences, or, if you believe someone else's response to your parenting is unhealthy, you may have to separate. Hopefully, differences can be discussed. I remember that I could allow my child to play with toy swords, and make toy guns out of toilet paper rolls, but I didn't feel comfortable buying him a commercially-made toy gun. I told him that, and he would say, "It's just a toy, Mom, not real. You can't really hurt people with this." But I had to express my feelings to him about guns, and why I did what I did. I had to acknowledge his very rational thinking about guns as well.

I talk to my clients having trouble with free expression and I always use the McDonald's restaurant example. When you have a serial gunman or random act of violence, they always describe the perpetrator as "such a quiet man. I never would have guessed it was him who did this!" It's not the free and openly expressive person who bottles everything up until he explodes and takes a bunch of people out.

In all walks of parenting life, you will see different forms of parenting and have your own ideas about it because people parent according to their own emotional growth and awareness, stemming from their background. Age also contributes to how we parent, provided emotional development has followed chronological development. As we learn more about life, we may become more flexible in our thinking and behavior — or at least so one hopes!

Mary and Ken are fearful and over-protective. Carl is too controlling and rigid, Donna has too many rules, Pam too few. Jack's family can't have cookies, Ellie's family has a snack drawer for after school. Lee gets to taste daddy's wine, Fred's parents think that's bad. Everyone's ideas come from their own view of parenting and how they want their child to be, and some think very little about what they're doing until it's called to their attention.

FOUR

Our Parents, Ourselves

I told her I hated the haircut. It was too short and I felt extremely ugly. She kept getting me the same short style, because it was summer, time for short hair. You didn't have long hair in the summer. It wasn't done."

Lack of emotional awareness:

"You're not afraid to take the chair lift. I've seen you do it before. Now get up there, and don't be a scaredy cat."

"I am too scared. I want you to come with me, please."

"You've done it before, now go; you don't need me. Everybody's waiting."

We learn to be emotionally aware in our lives first through our family experiences, and later, on our own, through life experiences and the people we meet. As you can see from the above examples, these parents didn't learn to be emotionally aware of their child's needs. They aren't listening to them either. Hopefully, somewhere along the line these parents will learn to respect their child's needs.

THE NEED FOR EMOTIONAL AWARENESS

Many people have had problems in their lives due to their upbringing and their parents' lack of emotional awareness in their parents, who come to counseling to learn how to express feelings, to accept feelings, and to feel happier and more connected. Some lack love or kindness, have low self-esteem, or are angry and disappointed in their lives. Some are depressed, lonely and anxious. Some just never learned how to listen to others, be there for them, and understand how their words and actions support, alienate, or control others. These folks, if they are capable, can look at themselves and grow enough that if they have children, they become more psychologically aware. When people aren't emotionally aware of others' needs, they also aren't aware of their own needs; through counseling, they learn to listen to their own feelings and therefore become more sensitive to others.

It's great for children when a parent gets help for themselves. A good therapist or mentor in one's life can help re-parent an adult, teaching the emotional awareness they originally missed out on and the non-productive thinking that came out of that lack of awareness. .

There are many detriments to the adult lacking in emotional awareness who is now parenting their own child. She may value things like control, discipline, and politeness, and desire a good child that behaves appropriately and does the right thing. She won't know, unless she seeks help, how to raise a feeling, emotive child who is free to express his/her own ideas and interests, who is capable of directing his or her thinking toward the productive, and who is respected and rewarded for that ability.

A parent's job is to help his/her children, teach them how to think, sponsor them, guide them, foster needs in them, and love them. In order to do this, the parent must refrain from the use of rigid words which attempt to control and force obedience, such as "Be good," "Don't run; don't play," and "By all means don't say that, it's bad and inappropriate."

As you become more enlightened and emotionally sensitive, you will notice the parents (who, by the way, love their child too), set the rules, the discipline. and the order, without the emotional awareness.

CHILDREN LEARN FROM YOU

Mutual expression of feelings from parent to child is the best way to grow your child emotionally, but if you're lacking in ability to express your needs, your helping yourself automatically helps your child. Once you begin talking more openly with your child, you will see the benefits of open, honest communication. Your child will mimic and learn from you and begin openly expressing his/her feelings, especially since you've shown them how. Most adults prefer a direct and honest friend rather than one who is indirect in their expression or unable to tell them how they feel.

"SHOULDS" CAN POISON ADULTHOOD

Joanna will be dressed appropriately and look clean, but not really have the fun of getting dirty, walking barefoot, jumping on a bed, or hanging her homemade artwork on the wall. Sometimes I see adults raised with money in their family, who were often offered opportunities to go to a good school, take riding or tennis lessons, but who now don't know what they want. They only know how they're supposed to be. Again, they value status and things rather than people and connection. They go to a school because that's what done and they never stop until they're older to think about what they wanted.

For example, I had one adult client, age thirty-four, who couldn't decorate her apartment with her own things because growing up she was told that tape would ruin the walls. Therefore, she couldn't hang up her artwork. Her mother also didn't want it cluttering up the refrigerator. Only real artwork was allowed on the walls. Her mother had an anxiety problem, and was herself raised to behave in an "appropriate manner," but my client didn't understand this until she received help. Now, at forty years of age, she has to let go of this story and learn to find who she is and what her tastes are. The parents picked out her dresses for parties, what school she would go to, and now, as an adult, she still needed her mother's approval and opinion. She couldn't trust her own judgment. She never learned how.

Jan's parents were under a great deal of stress. Her father was always working and Mom felt stressed alone with three kids much of the time. Mom, to quell her own anxiety, constantly kept her kids at bay by shushing them all the time and keeping them clamped down. They couldn't run in the house, or play too rough, and if they said a "bad" word she would overreact. She was nervous and anxious and this focused her on keeping order, rather than sponsoring her children's healthy development. She wasn't capable because she wasn't taught the skills. Jan developed an eating disorder, hid all her emotions, and secretly harbored a great deal of anger toward anyone who knew how to express themselves and get their needs met.

Dawn grew up with a mother who thought showing off or being the center of attention was just terrible. She made comments about parents who bragged too much about their kids and encouraged her kids to never brag. She encouraged them to always help others, yet she was constantly criticizing others with different ideas than hers and she taught this to her daughter — to criticize and to never shine. Negative thinking patterns are contagious. This mother lacked emotional awareness and self-esteem.

THE NEED FOR SELF-ESTEEM

I have always praised my children because I see them as separate from me. I would rave about anyone I admired as a person, and I admire my kids. What I see as praise, someone else may see as boasting. Praise your children. They deserve it and will grow from it and feel valued and loved. Make sure you use positive words like "terrific," "wonderful," and "absolutely." It's important, even if you don't like someone or if someone angers you, to watch what you say about them. Children will pick up on the negativity. Remember, negative thinking is contagious.

Many girls I've worked with who have had eating disorders grew up hiding their light, not allowing themselves to blossom or be successful. This created low self-esteem. Praising, admiring and getting really excited about your kids' accomplishments is okay, provided they're as excited as you are! It's important for parents to have their own lives and interests and not to live through their kids. Doing the latter can cause the parents a great deal of disappointment.

COMPASSION

When I was growing up there was a woman, Mrs. Ash, a mother of one of my group of friends, whom all the girls loved to be around. We loved to go to her house after school and anywhere else with her. She had three girls and loved them deeply, constantly praised them and accepted them. She asked them about everything and was curious about their lives and friends even when they were older and didn't want to tell her. I always admired her gentleness and ability to love her daughters outwardly so much. Years later, another mother of my friends died and we all, Mrs. Ash included, went to the funeral. After some glasses of fine red wine, we all opened up and asked her how she managed to be such a good mother. One of us said that she must have had a really supportive, loving mother, and she laughed. "Oh, no," she said, "just the opposite. My mother always needed to control us and criticize us and tell us what to do and how to be. Nothing was right, and I'm sorry she died before I had a chance to talk with her." She told us that she made a conscious effort to never treat her daughters the way she was treated. This is being emotionally aware. We all have the ability to change and become more emotionally aware, but first we need to treat ourselves with respect and emotional awareness.

I was once in California at a conference with my husband and we met a man from a group my husband was consulting with. This man lived in a beautiful area of Northern California and asked us to go for a hike with him. He was kind and gentle and very interesting. I had my baby with me at the time. The man was attentive and looked lovingly at the little guy. As we walked and talked some more, I asked him if he had children. He told me with sadness in his voice that he did but didn't see them because he made mistakes that he was trying to mend. He had spent years as a businessman in New York City spending time working and making money, getting to the point where he hardly saw his kids, never mind paying attention to their feelings. He didn't know how. It wasn't until he had long divorced and looked at himself and gotten re-married that he realized the loss he had experienced from putting his excessive work before the needs of his kids. He had tried to make amends, but his children were too angry, and he was now emotionally aware enough to understand that and let them come around. He was learning to nurture himself to deal with the loss.

Through his own exploration, he realized how he was parented and how that affected him as a dad. The wonderful thing about this man is that he was willing and open to change. That, in and of itself, takes emotional awareness. Many people never reach this point because they are in too much denial, or are fearful and defensive in their ways.

SAD CHILDHOOD PATTERNS

Often it takes a problem like depression, anxiety, physical illness, alcoholism, break-ups in marriages and other relationships, or death for people to realize how their past has affected them and make the necessary changes. People often arrive at a place where they look at the lack of emotional awareness in their lives and either grow from this realization, or stay stuck, unchanged.

"My father never asked me my opinion, he just told me how it is and what I should do. He never really heard me."

"My mother was too anxious to listen. Now I know her drinking was a way she medicated her anxiety and stress. No one in her family expressed their feelings either."

"My parents never outwardly expressed feelings of anger. They were quiet and polite, without reactions. They were quite formal. I never saw them kiss or hug."

"Intellectual ability was of utmost importance. We had to be smart, that was the bottom line."

"The house was always spotless and we were very well-dressed. But no one ever asked me about my day. In fact, no one really communicated to me as a person. Children were subordinates to be seen and not heard."

"I kept telling my mother I hated to go to my cousin's because Aunt Joyce yelled all the time. I always knew she just waved over my silly feelings and took me to Aunt Joyce's. My opinion didn't matter, I was only a child."

"My mother was very rigid about food. She constantly worried about my weight and told me when, what, and where to eat. I had lots of friends and wasn't unhappy. She thought I felt the same as her. Sometimes I think this is why I never knew as an overweight adult when I was hungry, because my mother controlled when we ate, not our stomachs."

"My family liked to call us well-behaved. Now, as an adult, I wish I could have been more free-spirited. I was too nice, too well-behaved. Kids just aren't that good! There wasn't much humor in my family. My parents talked at us, not to us."

"When I got hurt on the bus and told my Dad another boy hit me, he asked me what I did first. I was trying to get him to understand that I got hurt and was afraid of this kid, but he devalued my feelings and didn't even ask first if I was hurt."

In the last of the above examples, emotional awareness would have had Dad first identifying with the boy's feelings about being hit. "Wow, what happened? That must have hurt! Tell me what happened." Even if the boy provoked his attacker in some way, identifying with his feelings shows caring and concern. Later, investigate and discuss. Dad jumped to the conclusion that his kid was at fault. This devalues feelings again and contributes to low self-esteem.

BLAMING THE CHILD

I have an active grade-schooler who loves recess and playing sports. One year I got about five calls early on saying he was okay, but fell while catching a ball and hurt his head. I was asked to be available by phone if he needed to come home. Time passed and I never got another call. Then a call came on one of my few days off saying I might have to come home since he fell over backwards playing "capture the flag." I was furious when I thought of how rough and uncontrolled his playing must have been for him to hit his head, and now I had to drive forty miles home, ruining my free afternoon. When he got home I asked, "What happened? How fast were you running to fall down?" I began to get angry with him for playing so wildly. He became very angry at me, saying that I didn't even ask him what happened and that made him really angry. Someone accidentally barreled into him and hurt him this time, and I didn't ask; rather, I made an assumption. He was right to express his anger at that, and I commended him and apologized for my assumption.

Joanne always feared her daughter Rose was at fault in any situation. She would see another child crying and ask the mother what Rose did. Half the time, Rose had done nothing, but Rose was labeled a problem by a mother who was projecting her own insecurities onto her child.

Cindy went to visit Mrs. Paxton next door. "Don't pester her," said her Mom. "She may be busy now." Mom is trying to be polite (that nasty word!) to Mrs. Paxton, but the wording of her sentence makes her daughter feel like she's a burden, a problem, a pest. Mom might be better off to say, "Have fun, and say hello to Mrs. Paxton. If she doesn't answer, she may be out or asleep, so don't ring too many times okay? You don't want to wake her up. Bye, honey."

Ray came home from school and told mom that he had a really bad day. The teacher had scolded him for talking out loud and made him sit in the hall, and never came back to get him until the secretary called her. Mom's immediate response was, "What did you do in class to make Miss Fish so mad?" Again it would be more productive in sponsoring emotional development for mom to say, "Gee, that must have felt bad to be alone in the hall and be forgotten." This wording identifies with the child's feelings of feeling forgotten. Later, mom can investigate whether the teacher was fair or unfair.

Identifying with children's feelings requires listening, a very important skill in helping any child or person to feel more emotionally secure and being comfortable with having all sorts of feelings.

Remember, no matter how we were parented, there is the opportunity to change the pattern if our parents lacked emotional awareness, by helping ourselves. We as parents can have fun growing emotionally and learning to nurture ourselves, and thereby become better nurturers to our children.

In the following chapters we will discuss using emotional intelligence in specific problem areas, but first, let's take a look at emotional awareness in schools.

FIVE

Schools and Emotional Awareness

As a parent searching for a preschool for my active three-year-old son, I was very concerned about where he went. First, because I wanted teachers who had emotional understanding and awareness, and second, because I did not want my active boy to be labeled a behavior problem, as many active kids had been. I had seen too many parents and teachers try to squelch active energy with, "No, don't do that," "That's too wild," "Not okay," "Use your inside voice," and so forth. I was very afraid of having a teacher who had no humor, play, or ability to understand the energy of active boys teach my child.

I looked at a number of schools before finding a wonderful one, and I want to talk about some of the problems with emotional awareness that I found in the other schools I investigated.

Repressive Regimes

One school I visited had desks for three- and four-year-olds placed very close together, with little space to move. I asked the rather formal teacher where kids played on a rainy day when they couldn't go outside. She pointed me in the direction of a very small space and said, "This is where the children are allowed to run around. We really don't encourage running here." This is non-sponsoring of emotional development, because children run around. They have energy and love to play. Children run around. This is what they do. To discourage this lacks emotional awareness. It forces children into the "be quiet and polite" mode that often is enforced at the expense of emotional development. These are the words and ideas that go with children being controlled — well behaved at the expense of any sense of self.

Another school I visited had the children all dressed in buttoned-up shirts and ties. They told me not to worry, because they would be getting more computers in. Not one teacher spoke with my child at the open house, but the kids were neat and clean and knew how to use a computer. What about being a child, what about communication and nurturing? It wasn't happening here. All the kids were neatly appointed, and you could tell their mothers dressed them to fit the "appropriate" attire demanded by the school.

Teachers and schools without emotional awareness can be very harmful to kids. When rules, dress, or behavior is more important than knowing a child and working with who they are, there is a problem. The children will learn to conform, not to grow into their own person. At any age it is important to look at your school and the teacher's way of handling children.

The Right School

The preschool I ended up picking for my daughter had a huge bottom floor of a church for kids to play in winter and on rainy days when they couldn't get out. Children came in all kinds of clothes, and play and socialization were first and foremost. It wasn't unusual for a teacher to hold a child on her lap or until she felt comfortable when her parent left. Children felt respected and loved. There were rules, but the teacher explained the rules and why they existed. If a more active child was told to sit out or have a talk about his energy, the physical nature of the child was taken into account and worked with.

The same applied to a shy child, an overly aggressive child, or any other type of child.

THE INDIVIDUALITY OF CHILDREN

Sometimes adults who lack emotional intelligence feel there children should be a certain way, and if they're not that way they see something wrong in the child. It is important to remember that like adults, children have different levels of energy and different personalities, and they as little children are often too young to always control these things. It's not bad or wrong for one child to be athletic, one to be quieter, and another more outspoken or more bossy. Children need to be worked with, respecting their individuality and of course taught better ways when their behavior hurts another.

Let me give you an example of how my son's kindergarten teacher worked to know my son's own personal style.

When my son went to meet his kindergarten teacher, she asked him lots of questions, listened very carefully, and then asked him if he had ever used a balance board that she had in the classroom. She had lots of different play things that different children might like. You had to balance on this toy like a skateboard. She got on it and formed an instant connection to him through a physical move. This was emotional intelligence on her part in connecting to him. She picked up on what he liked to do by asking him questions and used that knowledge to connect to him.

As a therapist, I do this all the time with clients, even those really distressed with their symptoms of anxiety and depression. I find out what they like, what they do well in and what they'd like to do well in to better connect with them.

Emotional Awareness of Schools

So check the emotional awareness of the schools and school philosophies you are considering for your child. It's like looking for a job. There are environments where people respect individuals and value input, and so make sure you're valued and praised for your work, in contrast to other people who won't pay any attention to that. They will be more formal and may have rigid sets of rules. In these environments, certain types of personalities carry out these rules, often without any emotional insight or ability. It's important that teachers listen to children and express feelings freely with them so that they will sponsor intellectual, as well as emotional development.

I discussed in an earlier chapter how wonderful it was that a school like the Massachusetts Institute of Technology was so aware of the problems with lack of emotional intelligence or uneven social/intellectual development, that they developed the program called "Charm School" to help kids. A mock social dinner event was set up so that counselors could teach students how to strike up conversations, connect, and relate to others socially, not just intellectually. The school realized that kids have more advantages if they're bright intellectually and have the ability to relate to and express feelings with others. This makes for better people, employees, and managers.

Schools are major institutions where our children are educated intellectually and emotionally. It's very important, if you are concerned about your child's emotional development, to interview people at the school (be it private or public) and to listen to the officials and observe their emotional connection and their philosophy about the school's role in educating your child.

I was once looking at private schools for personal information, and I was amazed at the different styles and philosophies. One school played soft music in the classroom because they promoted the arts. On that particular week they were studying Latin America, so they played the music of those countries. The students came in singing to the music and moving around. The school had a big informal relaxed classroom with lots of group interaction and feedback.

Another school I looked at was extremely neat and organized. The kids sat formally in their chairs; definitely, no music was allowed, on the grounds that it would have been distracting. The children were lectured to, with no group interaction. It is very important, whether the school is strict or not so, to check the emotional awareness of the staff. Remember, by emotional awareness, I mean the connections that staff are able to create with kids. They have time to see them as individuals with needs and behaviors particular to them. They don't try to fit children who are square or rectangular pegs into their one round hole, their one way of doing things. If kids spend so much of their day in school, and emotional awareness and connection aren't present, the child will have trouble, unless the parents are making up for the school's deficits, and if the parents are unaware of the school's deficiency in this area, they probably are not making up for the loss.

I once took my daughter, at age five, to an art class and the teacher spoke to her and the other kids, ages five and six, as if they were stupid. She talked down to them in a very destructive way. "Now children, let's all put our supplies on our desk." Without even establishing eye contact or listening to them when they talked she went on and on talking to the air. One day in the car, my daughter explained that she didn't want to go to the class because the teacher talked as though she and the kids were stupid. I was amazed at this insight because I was having mixed feelings about the class, too.

We talked about how this teacher meant well but needed to stop talking down to the kids. The teacher did not respect the intelligence of her class. She didn't know, and was unaware, of how she was affecting children.

As a parent, when your child tells you something about a teacher, listen to them. Don't assume they are exaggerating, overreacting, or complaining about nothing. Listen to the children. They are our greatest teachers!

Let's move on to specific problem areas and how we can use emotional intelligence to respect children, help them grow, and end some needless struggles for control. In my examples, I speak often of young children because I believe it's best to start sponsoring emotional development early on, but these examples can relate to any age. As adults, we spend years trying to discover the self by peeling away the layers and layers of stuff we have learned emotionally to get to our core. Children are already there. Let's keep that core protected by soft, respecting layers.

Six

Emotional Awareness: Feeding

A s a therapist who has been working with food-related issues for twenty years, I can say that (1) diets do not work, and (2) forced feedings don't work. Most of us as adults need to get back to eating like children, on demand.

Children eat when they are hungry. Any parent who has watched their child eat two bits of breakfast or lunch knows this. Children also know what they don't like and refuse to eat what they don't like. They can be less flexible than adults. Kids have very different tastes; some will eat Thai food, while others want to live on a pizza/soda diet. This is all enough to drive you crazy until you learn to

81

become more emotionally aware and confident around your child's eating habits.

FLEXIBILITY IN FEEDING

Emotional awareness in this area is to be aware of your child's nutritional needs, and a basic knowledge is okay; too much sugar equals a bad night for parents, kids get wound-up. Pizza and soda every day isn't a great plan, but a parent can respect a child's tastes while trying to modify his/her diet with healthy available foods. Restricting a child who really wants something isn't a good idea because forbidding or restricting makes him want more. Any chronic dieter will tell you about the inflexible way they've eaten most of their life.

Forcing food on children is a no-no. Offering many healthy choices is good. Offering without huge expectations is even better. Let your child see you enjoying healthy food and feeling good about it, but also having a cookie or piece of cake freely. If you restrict or constantly obsess about food and weight, so will your child. Get rid of words that label salads good and cookies bad. Cookies aren't bad. Parents may think of their own anxiety around eating and weight gain as making them better parents to their children.

When children are allowed flexibility in meal planning and times to eat, they learn at an early age how to rely on their inner time clock. They listen to their inner messages of hunger rather than eating because the clock says so now.

What's more productive than forcing a child to eat breakfast, for example, because their bus is coming (since that will be creating anxiety around eating for them), is to say "What would you like for breakfast?" Let them choose their own food or pick from several of your ideas, and if they say they're not hungry, make food available and help them understand that they may get hungry so they need to take something with them. Most kids do survive until snack time just fine. If they don't take something with them, they'll feel what it's like to be hungry and be prepared next time. Their preparation will be self-initiated, and the goal will be to teach them to feed themselves.

ANXIETY AROUND EATING: DON'T PASS IT ON!

We need to relax ourselves around our children's eating. They will eat freely and naturally listen to their body's needs if not forced. Our guidance will be helpful. For example, Marsha, a thirty-six year old mother, had a weight problem most of her life. She was always on diets. She lost weight and became obsessed with everything she ate; no pizza, no junk or sweets, only natural foods. She looked great and shopped at the health food store. Then she had kids. She was constantly making them eat her health foods and became very nervous if she knew they would have soda or cake at a party. The kids picked up on her nervous energy around food. If you're relaxed and eat healthfully, that message will carry over to your children. If you are obsessed with weight, food and dieting, that message will also take root in your children; they can develop eating disorders.

Offering fruit and health foods is great, if not done out of restriction, anxiety and control. If you are a parent who is anxious around your own food and weight, get some help for yourself in becoming more flexible and curbing anxiety and fear, or else you will promote it in your children.

We want children and adults to make healthy choices, not to eat an apple because a piece of candy or two is bad. A little candy never ruined anyone's life! It's the labeling of food, the restriction that causes the problem. If you offer your children freedom in eating and having a relaxed attitude, there's no restriction to rebel against. You will set the stage for healthy and easygoing eating, and thus fewer problems with obesity and eating disorders.

Offer choices and flexibility in eating. If you eat something "bad" as an adult, change that language, forgive yourself and move on. Make a healthier choice tomorrow.

It's also helpful to watch your language regarding weight

and body image in front of children. Children are smart and they pick up on your views of yourself. Even if you as a parent have to lose weight, you can be positive in your approach to it rather than judgmental about yourself. By being positive about your own weight loss, you will give your child the language to be hopeful and positive. For example, "I'm really enjoying food recently and need to make some healthier choices for myself, so tonight we'll have fresh vegetables, homemade soup and bread and I'll skip the cake for tonight. It looks delicious though; have a piece." If you are positive and light about yourself, your kids will emulate that. Here's the flipside.

"I'm getting really fat and eating too much fat. Look at how fat I am. I need to cut this junk out and so do you kids. No more candy or sweets in the house. I'm going to blow up and you'll get fat too!" We may feel this way, but it's not a productive way to think or behave.

I worked with a mother who was very thin and constantly watching her diet, and complaining she was fat. She was five feet seven inches and weighed about 120 pounds, far from fat. Her daughter would hear her and say "Mom, you're not fat at all," and the mother would deny it. Well, the daughter was, though not overweight, heavier for her than the mother. So what's the message to the daughter? "You are fat too." The mother learned through her work on herself how she was promoting a poor body image and a possible eating disorder.

Listen to kids, help them to respect their bodies, and give them guidance and support toward eating well. For example, Jenna was very thin, ate only healthy foods, but constantly criticized her height, weight, and shape of her stomach. Her daughter, watching this, may learn to evaluate her body negatively. Complain if you'd like, but not in front of your child. It isn't good to evaluate bodies in front of children.

I worked with a family whose daughter related that her mother called people on one television show "fat." "My mother's obsessed about my weight and diet," she said. The mom eventually learned to back off and not to teach her child to be obsessed with weight or make fun of overweight people. Again, emotional development is conscious parenting — that is thinking about how what you do and say affects your kids.

Another mother I worked with had lost a great deal of weight after her divorce. She had worked hard to diet, and became a personal trainer. However, because she lost weight, she projected all her feelings around weight onto her teenage daughter. Mom became obsessed with her daughter's weight, and constantly tried to manage her eating, which in turn caused resentment and weight gain in the daughter. Again, emotional awareness means helping, accepting, teaching, not controlling. This mother needs to see herself separately from her daughter.

Remember, children do live what they learn!

As a side note, remember that kids are kids and they

have different tastes than adults. Try to accommodate their tastes, adding ingredients that you think they might like and may have more protein. For example, keep trying different things and they'll see you trying choices in an easy, relaxed way. Try different foods yourself and let them know the good things, such as certain vitamins and minerals, which certain foods offer. You will work toward creating a child whose body tells him/her what it needs, and this is a very good thing.

SEVEN

Emotional Awareness: Bedtime

The struggle at bedtime can begin early and travel into adolescence. As any parent knows, children are experts at avoiding bedtime and sleep. It's Baba the bottle when they're younger, water, a night light, a ghost, a kiss, another kiss, a story, a pain, a noise . . . and the list goes on. It can drive you mad!

Here are some emotional awareness questions to ask yourself about bedtime. Are your kids tired when they go to bed? If they can't fall asleep, should you adjust bedtime? Do you give younger kids a bottle? Can they sleep without one? If you don't give one and they want it, why did you not give it? What is the reason?

For example, I knew two women with small children,

ages three and four, who still wanted juice before bed in a bottle. One woman refused to give it to the child even though she cried for a good forty-five minutes past bedtime without it. The other woman gave it to her child, feeling intuitively that she would give it up when she was ready. Emotional awareness would allow the child to have the bottle until she was ready to give it up. Pulling a security object away from a child isn't necessarily a good thing, and you have to think about whether this evening bottle is really hurting this small child. When you are emotionally aware or have developed more emotionally, you will learn to rely on your intuition more and the advice of experts less. If you agree with the experts, that's fine, but sometimes people follow the expert because they can't rely on their own judgment.

RULES: ARBITRARY OR REASONABLE?

I remember a pediatrician telling one of my clients that when her child was two, she should immediately pull him off the bottle. I think sometimes these rules are made arbitrarily without giving credence to the needs of the child. We all get stuck in the "shoulds" rather than using our intuition, common sense or the child's messages. Not every child should do certain things at the same time. Emotional awareness leads to more independent thinking.

Again, think about why you do or say certain things to your child. Why is your rule a rule?

It is important to set limits with kids around bedtime or you will be up with them all night, but again set them with an assertive tone and explanation. For example, saying, "It's nine o'clock now; you really need to go to bed because you have to catch the bus early and be rested for school," is very different than, "Go to bed now. It's your bedtime, and I said so." You can still feel angry when your children are stalling at bedtime, but express why you are angry openly. "You need to go to bed because you'll be too tired to wake up and catch the bus and I can't drive you to school. Go to bed please."

Now, mind you, as parents, having the toughest job around, we all slip and forget the emotional awareness part every so often We're human, tired, annoyed. But at least we can know what's more productive and can try to practice it more often.

It is better to explain a rule assertively than to arbitrarily command.

If you have a child who refuses to go to bed, saying they're not tired, use emotional awareness to give them some choices. Again, this will require some emotional development in the parent to be flexible to this idea. Maybe you can buy a booklet and let your child read in bed until they fall asleep. Most kids will eventually fall asleep. If the child stays up too late in bed reading, doing a puzzle, or playing with a handheld electronic game, it's not the worst thing for them to experience be-ing really tired in the morning and having to deal with it. Many kids learn this way to go to bed earlier, and may even ask to go to bed, listening to their inner time clock.

Soothing The Night Owl

Many parents do try too hard, at their expense and that of others, to try to strictly control bedtime. If you can get your child to bed and to sleep at 8:00 P.M., more power to you, but sometimes this seems impossible or at least extremely difficult without undue force! Emotional awareness means recognizing your child's habits and sup-porting them as long as they don't infringe on others' time. Teaching the night owl how to read or draw in bed to fall asleep is awareness. It also teaches them how to soothe themselves and respects their feelings.

Remember, as adults we may have one night when we're in bed at 9:00 P.M., and another night where we're up until 2:00 A.M. watching bad movies or reading a book. Children have different time clocks, too, and we need to respect that.

Be aware and flexible, and express your needs to your kids as a parent. For example, if your kids won't settle down and keep waking up, let them know now is your "alone time" or adult time, and they need to go to bed and respect your need for this time. Most children understand this. Showing your child that you have needs is a very positive thing. It teaches them to respect their own needs.

SLEEPING WITH PARENTS

Sometimes younger children will want to sleep in their parents' bed; this is common. Animals often like to join this sleeping arrangement as well.

Think about your flexibility in this area. Why do you say no? If you say, "No, I don't want you in my bed, get in yours," that sends a negative message.

"Daddy and I need more time to ourselves tonight as grown-ups," or "I need to stretch out alone tonight," or "I want to watch a grown-up movie" — this kind of language explains that they are wanted but, yes, you have needs. Letting children sleep with you periodically isn't a bad thing. In fact, it can be the most wonderful thing in the world!

Remember, tone of voice is important in communicating with anyone. Shouting, "I need to be alone!" doesn't send a supportive, "I have needs" message. It sends a "go away," arbitrary command message.

If you think about the way you accept, talk and interact with your kids, you will become aware of your own stress level. For example, one mom I worked with said to me, "I'm stressed to the max. I'm with them all day and then they stay up all night and come into my bed. I scream at them and think of a punishment." She learned to manage her stress better and be a more assertive parent.

Even if, for example, you choose never to let your kids sleep with you, you can convey this in a way that exhibits emotional awareness, rather than rejection. The same applies for taking a bottle away from an older child. For example: "I need the space to sleep guys. That's why I bought you those cool bunk beds. Come on I'll tuck you in." This is an assertive but kind way of expressing your need for alone time. The dad might say, "Guys, this bed is too small and you know how important sleep is for me. It's tough for me to get up when I don't get sleep, but let me lie with you for a minute."

Give Your Reasons

In discussing taking away a bottle from an older child, provided you feel it's the right thing to do, think about why you're taking it away and explain your reasons to your child in the best age-related terms. For example, "Honey, I know you want the bottle, but I feel it's bad for your teeth and would like you not to have it." "Let's fall asleep to a story tonight." "Here's a cup of juice for you." Let them know as people why you can't give them the bottle, and help them find another way to go to sleep. They may cry, but if you keep reassuring them, they will eventually go to sleep and at least know why you are saying no. Even at this young age, you have opened the lines of mutual concern, honesty and expression. This is a very different approach than, "You don't need a baba, you're too big now, only babies have bottles."

I don't think you can go wrong with openness and honesty. I do believe that children will naturally give up things when they're ready, and that's different for different kids. Respect that.

Remember, our goal as parents is to teach our kids through open communication to understand their needs and the needs of others. In regard to bedtime, our goal is to help them know sleep is important to get in order to function productively in their lives. Our goal is to help our children and listen to their inner time clocks telling them they're tired and need sleep. If a child isn't tired at all, then you can come up with the creative ideas to help them fall asleep or learn to soothe them.

As they get older, they will present many challenges, such as e-mailing until all hours of the night, hanging out in Internet chat rooms, and talking endlessly on the phone. Open communication, starting early in the child's life, allows you as the parent to promote mutual respect, which will ease the upcoming wars that occur between parent and child. Even if your children don't always follow your advice, and it's no surprise that sometimes they won't, you will have given them the emotional connection and respect they need to grow into happy, healthy, connecting adults.

"As an adult I look back at my mother. I love her as an adult so much and I wish she had told me how she felt when I was a child. She was so busy raising us in the way she thought a parent should, that she missed opening up to us. I missed out on getting to know a lot about her."

Anonymous client

EIGHT

Emotional Awareness: Dressing

Dressing is another area where a battle of wills can present itself. Now, mind you, some kids are easier and will wear whatever you want them to with no problem. Kids have different personalities, and the perfect kid may be different from the kid who exercises his or her will regularly.

I don't really believe that there are any perfect kids. I hope not, yet some really have natures that make them more compliant even without the parents' help in controlling what their kids do.

YOUNGER CHILDREN'S DRESS

For example, I met one mother who had a set idea of how her boy should dress. She really liked the preppy look, and he wore it. He didn't find a need to pick out his own clothes. Had he, this would have posed a problem for the mom, who insisted she should pick out his clothes. She would have either had to force him to wear an outfit or offer more flexibility.

I think it's good for children to exercise choice. I also think kids know at a very young age what they like, how they want their hair, their pants, and so forth. We especially see the older kids, seven and up, being very conscious about what they're wearing. Again, there are exceptions to the rule, but I think they are rare. Dressing is part of socializing, of being accepted by the child's culture.

My children knew very early on what they wanted to wear, and I let them pick, but made that picking manageable so that I didn't lose my mind. I didn't say, especially at age three and four, "Go pick whatever you want," because I knew this was an all-day affair. Instead, I got an idea of their style and gave them two or three choices already put together. My son, who was easy, said, "That's a cool pair of pants, but could you get me another shirt?" He had only three, though they were in the same style he really liked. My daughter was much more difficult, saying she didn't like my choices. I'd ask her what she liked or didn't like and set a limit on when she needed to be ready. If she wasn't ready, I'd get ready to leave and let her know I needed to leave to be somewhere at a certain time. She'd sometimes kick and scream but would find an outfit. I'd always tell her I was sorry she was so angry, but she had to get dressed in time for school and couldn't hold everyone up. I suggested later that she plan her outfit the night before and offered my help.

Sometimes a child will pick an outfit that really looks silly to us as a parent. Let them be creative as long as they're not going to school in a loincloth. Letting them choose will teach them to value their individuality and make choices. It is a good thing.

DRESS PROBLEMS WITH OLDER CHILDREN

Older children may present more of a problem because their bodies become more developed, and certain choices may seem really inappropriate to you as a parent. One of my clients told me that she had gone to a private school that had a dress code, and that she switched over to public school in eleventh grade. She told me what kids were wearing on the first day of school, and all I could do was to picture my daughter in about five years. Bustiers, MTV outfits, midriffs hanging, pierced everything . . . wowee!

If we talk about emotional intelligence here, we must respect our children's world and how they are growing up, but also let them know that as parents we love them, and explain why we advise against wearing a certain outfit, such as a feathered boa bustier with matching skirt. Again, if we tell them it's not appropriate, that it looks cheap or tawdry, it makes them feel bad or pushes them to rebel against us, which they do anyway in their teens — it's their job. However, I do believe that we can let them know how we feel and hopefully influence their decision by letting them know why we're suggesting that they not wear the bustier outfit. "You know it shows so much of you, and it's better not to wear that type of thing to school because someone might notice too much of your body and not enough of you!" You can say this assertively, but humorously, and make them think.

Make sure though, if the outfit isn't like the one mentioned above, that you're not imposing your judgment on them. Telling a kid baggy pants make him look unattractive and messy when all their friends are wearing them as the style isn't letting them be who they are. They have their whole life to wear suits and pantyhose; let's not rush it! Let them be free while they can! Watch out what you criticize and why.

Remember that it's important for us as parents to pick our battles. Kids will wear things that we see as ugly, dirty, too risqué, inappropriate for the occasion and unflattering to their bodies, but, believe me, they will outgrow it, and you need to respect their tastes. They are teenagers because they dress and act as they do. They are not adults. They are a different species! Respect their need for creativity and independence. It will help them immensely.

How We Were Dressed

When we look at how we parent around certain issues such as our kids' way of dressing, we can't help but reflect on how we were parented. It is good for us as parents to look at how we felt when our parents talked about our way of dressing. Were they supportive? Did they compliment us on our style? Did they allow us to make choices (and why, why not?) Often, our own children help us to grow emotionally as people because we are forced to look at ourselves.

I remember as preteens, in my day, (the late 60's) our parents forbade us to wear dirndl skirts to school. These were short, short skirts, gathered at the waist by elastics. We would roll them up, place them in our purse and put them on in the girls' room at school with shoes way too high for our mothers' liking. This was our trademark. This short little skirt was part of who we were.

OPEN-MINDEDNESS
IN DRESSING YOUR CHILD

Emotional awareness in parenting requires open-mindedness, a questioning of our ways or rules and why they were made. Emotional awareness means opening up to see that our view of the world and how it should be is not everybody's view. If we have a child who really thinks tattoos are beautiful and wants one, we can explain why we don't want them to get one, but not overlook their feeling that a tattoo is really beautiful. Hey, some adults think they are too. Just think — it might say "MOM." That would be an honor!

Certain types of dress define kids' identity. For example, one of my young clients lives in a small suburban town, where most high school kids look like 60's throwbacks or jocks. There are lots of baggy pants, and the girls have pierced noses, scarves, long hair, and tattoos. At another client's school, the girls dress more conservatively and somewhat sexily, with tight designer clothes and acrylic nails. My client that dresses in acrylic nails, and tight clothing, isn't trying to act sexy. She is doing what her friends do, and actually will not notice her midriff is completely exposed until someone makes a comment. She isn't quite aware of how others view the skimpy clothing. This is good and bad. Good because of her body image, and bad because she has no idea of the trouble she could get into. The parent is challenged once again. How do we get the message across to dress more conservatively, yet not criticize or condemn her choices. Too much control of dress could make her feel self-conscious or bad about her body, or rebellious to the point of wearing less clothing! It would be better to compliment her looks, followed by an explanation of why it might be in her best interest to change.

Mary had a very strong memory of being a kid and getting ready for church. She came down in a black turtle-neck and an Indian skirt and her mother told her to change because the outfit wasn't appropriate for church.

Mary remembers telling her mother, "God doesn't care what I am wearing, you do." Her mother still made her change, and got angry with her for arguing about this. She missed the opportunity to sponsor my independent thinking, because she was too concerned with her idea of appropriateness. People have different ideas of what's appropriate.

Listen to your kids; respect their choices and self-direction. You'll be glad you did in the long run.

NINE

Our Busy Lives: Kids and Activities

PARENTS NEED A LIFE, TOO

Sometimes we can get so wrapped up in the day-to-day hassles of life that we forget to stop in the moment to practice the Zen nature of just being. We are so pressured in today's world to do, to be, to accomplish, and to do so quickly. We are so stressed by money, time, and the fear of aging that we forget to take time to be in the moment.

We need to slow down and consciously think about our actions and words and how they help our children or hinder their emotional growth. For example, we need to remind ourselves to slow down, look kids in the eyes, and ask them about their day. This should be with full attention, not thinking about a phone call, a play date, or food in the oven. We need to make time as parents for our children, but also for ourselves and significant others. Parents need a life too, or they end up resentful and old before their time. We need to talk and keep a listening ear even if our children reject it; they still want it and feel loved by it. If we are constantly doing, going, and doing more and more, we don't have the time to talk and listen to ourselves or our children.

I know sometimes I'll be so busy, I'll forget that my little girl has been asking me to play with her. Later I think to myself, what was more important, checking that message which I knew wasn't that important, or taking a moment to sit with her and play, because she's what really matters to me? Sometimes we have to force ourselves to play things we don't want to. Play it anyway, and make it time-limited to ease the torture! Sometimes we forget what's most important to us until something reminds us. I was reminded of this recently when my dog was hit by a car. He broke his leg and was in a collar, but he was alive! It was easy to think about how much work and money he would be, but I had to remind myself how fortunate we were that he was still alive. He was also a pain in the ass alive, but when I thought about never seeing him or lying down with him it was awful.

Emotional intelligence means extending it to yourself too, not just to your children. Parents need to be aware of their needs, the need for time together, time alone, time to take care of health, in order to be healthier parents. The more positive strokes we give to ourselves, the more we will give to our children. If we allow ourselves to be free, we will allow our children the same.

It is important to seek happiness for ourselves, so that our words and actions will have a positive impact on our children. I once had a client whose dad never really loved his job, was very stressed and unhappy, and who would constantly complain about work. He was a physician, and a very unhappy one. At age thirty-three, my client was unfulfilled, particularly in her work life. She was a bright woman, but would take menial jobs that didn't require much commitment because she didn't want to be tied to a horrible job her whole life. She had difficulty as an adult feeling good about work or believing that it could be fun because she heard negative messages from her dad constantly when she was growing up. Her work in counseling was to change this programming and real-ize her work could be enjoyable and rewarding if she so chose. Her father had that choice, too. He was just wrapped up in messages from his past, and an inability to change thinking.

Be careful what you say; your words will create a reality for your child. If you as a parent are unhappy, how could you change your situation?

Another client with whom I worked had a father who always spoke in an angry, sarcastic tone. You would say

"Good morning." and he would negatively joke, "What's good about it, roar, roar." Her dad was under so much stress and carried so much anxiety that he couldn't relax and calm himself down. Subsequently, my client was anxious around her work and often worked too much and too hard, taking out her stress on everyone around her. Because she had grown up with angry language and stressful behavior, it was hard for her to meet relaxed people who treated her kindly. Not until she had the courage to change her thinking and actions did her life change. Think about words; they leave a lasting effect.

If You Relax, Your Child Will Relax

The parents in these examples were stressed from too much work and too many demands. It's very important for kids to see parents slowing down and getting their needs met. If the parent neglects her own needs, the child will learn not to value their own without some help. The parents need to be taught how to think more effectively.

As parents, it is helpful to look for ways to find relaxation and to slow down in this busy and stressful world. There are so many opportunities available today — yoga, meditation, parent support groups, newcomers' clubs in town — where people can meet other parents and connect if they're feeling isolated and alone. Being with people for support as a parent is very important for mental health and emotional nurturing. When children are encouraged by parents to have fun, to relax and talk with friends, they will do the same. Remember, children do as we do.

This brings me to the new wave of kids and activities.

OVER PROGRAMED CHILDREN

I like to joke that my eleven-year-old son has done more in his short life than I've done in a lifetime! Most kids nowadays are enrolled beginning at age four in different activities. Parents take them to soccer, tee-ball, karate, gymnastics, prima ballerina training, math camp, hockey, more and more and then some. When I was eleven years old, my only worry was whether a neighborhood kid was around to play with in their yard, or where to buy a playing card to attach to my bike for a cool sound effect. Occasionally, we walked to the corner store to buy rat fink rings. Now kids are practicing for tournaments and trying out for higher league after higher league.

Parents' emotional awareness and intelligence is tested here, because you can really get wrapped up and anxiety-ridden in this shuffle. "Will my kid be behind if he doesn't go to eight-hour soccer camp?" "Cindy's daughter takes ballet, should I send Anna? What if she's not athletic? What if my son isn't, will he be left out?" "Who's around this summer? Everyone goes to camp. I don't think we can afford that." And the anxiety goes on. Parents can become competitive and over-stressed.

Emotional awareness means knowing when enough is enough and when your kids seem okay with the activities in their lives. This means not letting competitions and busy schedules rule your life. Learn to become consciously aware if your child looks tired and needs to take a break. You would be surprised at the pushing some parents do, with little regard for their child's feelings or condition. They are unaware. I see this all the time in sports. The dad is yelling at the kid to perform, perform, perform, and the kid looks as though he'd rather be anywhere but there. Be aware of the messages you send your child and how much you push them to meet your needs. The sports nut may end up having a kid who can't stand the pressure and doesn't want to use his/her talent because he or she was pushed too hard.

FORCING YOUR CHILD'S GIFT

For example, one of my clients enrolled her five-year-old in ballet class. She really felt this activity would benefit her child. She felt ballet was graceful and disciplined and good training for her daughter. She signed her up for a ten-week class, and her daughter had a difficult time each time they went. She didn't feel comfortable in the class and was very shy. This was a formal school, parents weren't supposed to stay in the class, and the child had trouble when Mom left. The teachers were very formal rather than nurturing.

The child would report to mom that the steps were too hard and that she felt shy and uncomfortable. The mother kept insisting she stay in class because the mother had paid money for it. The mom especially wanted her daughter to continue when she spoke to a friend with an older daughter who told her that her daughter's first year was hard, but after that, she loved it and now is excellent at ballet. This mom's competitive nature kicked in, and instead of thinking of her child's individual needs, she kept doing what she felt was appropriate: teaching her child discipline.

To give my client credit, she was concerned about whether she was doing the right thing. She didn't want her daughter to learn to be a quitter, but was this feeling exaggerated in her due to her own upbringing? Could her daughter be her own person even at age five?

The mother, through work on herself, realized that her daughter hadn't liked structured play, and was still quite shy when not with Mom. The mom learned to recognize this as part of who her daughter was, not something problematic or wrong. This is what knowing and respecting your kids as people is about. The mother saw her daughter as a five-year-old unaware of what she needed;

she saw her as a child in need of the mother to push her, to be strong.

Through counseling, the mom learned to listen to her girl rather than rule out her feelings. She learned that it was okay to quit ballet. Maybe she'd like it as she got older, so she asked for her money back for the unused sessions. She had been hesitant to do this, seeing it as impolite. Several months later, her daughter enrolled in a kid's gym program and loved it from the start. It was much different from the structured ballet class. It had free, open play, parents could watch, and it was an informal friendly atmosphere.

My daughter is nine, and at four she told me she felt too young to do anything other than play at home. She's very clear on birthdays that she only wants a small group because for her, too many is overwhelming. She is very clear on her feelings. I don't force her to change them.

WHEN UNFAIRNESS LEADS TO ANGER

Another mom I worked with brought her eight-year-old son in for counseling. "He is very athletic and energetic," she said. "Sometimes he just gets really wild and out of control, and it's so embarrassing." She described an example when the boy was playing basketball and the coach set it up so he had to pass to a boy who really wasn't a very good player. The lesser-skilled boy kept missing the ball, and subsequently, despite all my client's son's great effort, the other team creamed them. At the end of the game, her child kicked and screamed, angry at how unfair this was. He kept yelling that the other boy couldn't play well. This was a kid who usually would carry the ball by himself and score because he was so determined and athletic, but his coach taught him to pass. Passing is good, it's teamwork, but if you give 150% and you're teamed with a player who can't play it is frustrating, and an eight-year-old can't reason like an adult. They want to win. They are frustrated. Actually, an adult would be frustrated by this.

When this woman's son would become angry, people would stare at her and her son as though they had two heads. No one seemed to be aware of the age of this kid and his frustration at the setup and its justification. His feelings were not acknowledged.

I encouraged the parents to talk to the coach, explain the situation and not set this kid up to get so angry. As adults we can reason, talk to the coach, and ask for a different arrangement in players, but an eight-year-old usually can't do this. They react with emotion to the un-fairness and disappointment. It's normal, not a problem.

We need to work with the energy of kids and understand it, not set them up to be labeled a problem.

David, a ten year old, was invited to a soccer party with

a group of boys. Most kids are playing a game of soccer to win, and most athletic kids really want their team to win. The "no competition and have fun" attitude is often the parents' influence, not the kids' desire. Kids like to win.

Anyway, the birthday boy and his team were already set up to win at this place, because you can't let the birthday boy lose, right? The problem is, they picked my son to be captain of the losing team; however, he played to win with his teammates, having no idea that it was a set-up. When the other team fell behind, they'd give them the point, and my son was a wreck by the end of the game. He had worked really hard, only to have points not counted or handed to the other team. He reacted with crying, anger, shouting "Unfair!" and when I came to the party, to get him, only a few parents and coaches were aware of his frustration. The kids were not taken seriously. Emotional awareness is the exact opposite of setting kids up in this way. The set-up was unfair. I made an effort to talk to the people at the party and explain the effects this has on young children. They listened. They were unaware of how their actions affected intelligent kids.

The more we educate parents, teachers, and people in general about the necessity of being emotionally aware, the better our lives and our children's lives will be.

In a world so busy with work and events, it is very important to take time to feel, to listen, to relax and slow down.

TEN

Toward a New Psychology of Being

It is clear that there is a need in our world for more emphasis on emotional awareness and development. Many work toward this — the human resources people who go into companies to help their employees to become more psychologically aware, humorists who make light of the seriousness we all show toward power and control, and others who strive to bring people more in touch with themselves and their feelings.

It is so important to sponsor this emotional awareness in children, because they will not only become more whole individuals, but they also will become leaders who possess more than an excellent resume. We will have leaders who know that valuing people, praising them and rewarding them for good work makes them more productive because they feel valued and heard. Lacking emotional development in an organization repeats a family cycle of emotional neglect. When employees and teachers aren't heard by their bosses, they feel bad and under-valued. Their motivation lessens and they don't feel good in their positions. We must do our own part to stop this by working on ourselves and others close to us.

LACK OF EMOTIONAL AWARENESS

As a therapist, I hear stories all the time that confirm the lack of emotional awareness in our world. A man comes in, he's worked for a company for nine years, and without notice he's given a warning that if sales don't improve he's out. Another client walked into work to the door of her boss that said "Do not disturb." He was cold and professional in his manner at all times. A woman is told her daughter is too shy and will have problems, and to consult a psychiatrist. Someone is told their active son has ADD and is too difficult, without respecting his energy. People decide intellectually what's appropriate and what isn't, and listen to others without question. Some doctors' offices are curt and cold on the phone, and people often wait for their appointment endlessly without even a face to come out and apologize. But people do it. People are told that they have only one vacation a year and God forbid you need more time off. Many would not dare to ask. I recently dealt with a well-known psychiatrist in my area of specialty, who, because he felt he had rank, did a disservice to a patient and was dismissive of my ideas. This happens all the time, and we need to learn to value ourselves, to speak up and promote change in these kinds of behavior.

When I assisted a career counselor in my late twenties, I was shocked to see how many people were changing careers at age forty-five and up. I always had suspected the group would be younger. But now, in my mid-forties, I understand it often takes age to gain emotional awareness and to be in touch with our selves, our true desires and needs. It takes skill and time as people to admit that we have made mistakes, and could afford to change our behaviors and actions. That's why it's so great to teach our children this awareness when they're so young.

The Benefits of Life Experience

The experiences we have in life will most often contribute to our free self-expression. We eventually realize life doesn't go on forever and think about how we want to live it, as opposed to how we should live it.

Many of us have seen elderly people say exactly what's on their mind like children. I believe it's because nothing really surprises them; they're older and wiser.

I once worked at a hospital rehabilitation program, and when I came back to visit, the social workers told me a humorous story about an elderly retired man, a therapist/minister who was volunteering in the rehab. The young psychiatrists in charge of the meeting, meeting would say things that to him made little sense, sometimes because they were young and needed to gain experience emotionally and intellectually. He'd freely disagree, always being kind, but making it clear he thought the idea was not necessarily helpful in this case. The staff loved him because he said all the things they wanted to say but couldn't. They were too busy being "appropriate"! They were embarrassed to speak in the group or speak up to a superior. Unfortunately a lot of this assertive ability, lack of fear, comes with age. But life is short. Let's help speed up the process of free thinking in our children. Then they won't have all the shoulds that prevent them from valuing their opinion.

I always learn from older people because they have seen it all and know that life is short. Most are not hung up on appearances and appropriateness. If they are, it's a shame that they are spending their years this way and that they haven't grown emotionally over the course of time. However, anyone can change at any time. I have many elderly people in my practice trying to change their thinking for a better, more fulfilled life with themselves and their children. I encourage them, no matter what their age to direct their lives where they want it to go now, as if life went on and on. Life is about insight, acceptance, growth, and change.

A NEW PSYCHOLOGY OF BEING

A new psychology of being means learning through your family, friends, role models, therapy, and experiences to become more open and honest and accepting of yourself, and therefore of your children. Let them grow into who they want to be, guiding them and sponsoring them all the way. When you discipline, be open in stating your reasons and do the same when you praise and encourage them. Teach them to be free in their feelings and you will offer them the greatest gifts of all — self-esteem, free expression, accountability, and the ability to make positive decisions with ease. They will trust in themselves and their decisions.

When we become freer and more emotionally aware, we are more flexible, tolerant, objective and empathetic with ourselves and others.

INTELLECTUALISM VS. EMOTIONAL GROWTH

I think back to my many years as a therapist. When I first started I was controlling, feeling I had to have all the answers for the clients. I had a lot of "shoulds" and "shouldn'ts" running through my head. Now, twenty years later, I am a much different person and therapist. I learn probably as much from my clients as they do from me. I am more open, more able to listen, less self-righteous and in need of all the answers. I ask questions, and if I am challenged I try and ask questions, and don't judge. I ask question often, and evaluate my own behavior and actions to see where they need adjusting. I listen so that I can learn where people come from. What made them into who they are today? I have realized that the field of psychology is pursued by some as an intellectual endeavor, but effective counseling comes from connection, intuition, love, and common sense. This isn't usually taught in school. You learn about protocol, how to do research, diagnosis, and labels and appropriate referrals — all necessary things, but valueless without the emotional component.

Years ago, I decided to pursue a doctorate and visited a program. I sat in on a day-long class at a reputable institution. The teacher was a well-known psychologist. He was clearly in charge of the group in a commanding and controlling way, and I marveled at how in awe everyone was of him. No one seemed free to speak their mind, but instead looked for approval, which was tough to get.

A man in the group in his late fifties, compared to most in their thirties and forties, was having trouble doing the homework because he had received a doctorate in the late 1960's and was told he needed to repeat a doctoral program since so much time had elapsed and he hadn't kept up a practice and a license. He was having trouble doing another four-year stint, and expressed his difficulty openly with humor to the group. He wanted to know if any credit could be given for the past doctorate. I liked this man's spontaneous nature, real personhood and connection. He was clearly a bit rebellious, an independent thinker trying to find an alternative and asking for one.

The group was rigid, unforgiving, and serious. No one empathized with him, especially the big cheese, but explained to him the handbook rules. They admonished him for his anarchist ways. "Those are the rules, and that's the way it is," they said. They were like the rigid controlling parents, lacking humor and scolding a child.

As I looked around the room at this scene I wondered, "If I had a problem, would I go to any of these people to get better?" Out of twenty-two people in that room, the answer was clearly "No." They knew their theories and their intellectual jargon and how to cram everything into their portable computers, but little about connecting to others and being open to new ideas. Even if their answer to him was no, you can't get any credit for the past, they could have been open and respecting of his idea.

Too much of the world runs this way because emotional intelligence is learned and many, despite their degrees and credentials, have not learned what it is.

We can learn about it from our children. We need to learn if we don't know how to listen to the wisdom they have to offer us. We need to respect their ideas and interests and sponsor and guide them, not control them.

If we learn to trust and love ourselves as parents, to have faith no matter what sort of lemons life throws us, we will teach the same to our children. They will learn to be open, honest people and secure in this life, despite the roller-coaster ride life throws us on sometimes when we're not looking.

Eleven

How Can We Change?

We change as parents, as people, by learning about ourselves, by paying conscious attention to our words and actions. Counseling, meditation, a personal coach, yoga, reading books like mine, religious institutions, and mentors are all potential pathways to change, self- realization, and introspection.

Is your thinking generally open, positive, and flexible, or does it need work? Are you positive with your children, most of the time? Remember, children live what they learn. How many have heard their child repeat verbatim something negative they said and cringed? They copy us; we are their mirrors.

Remember, children do as we do, not as we say.

PRODUCTIVE THINKING

Positive, productive thinking is learned, and most people's problems can be linked to irrational, non-productive thinking learned from past experiences. Therapists, particularly those called cognitive therapists, actually teach people to consciously control their thoughts, therefore their emotions. They teach people how to recognize negative thought patterns, challenge them, and incorporate new, more positive, rational thoughts into their minds. Emotional awareness is connected to positive, healthy thinking. Try new things in life yourself so that your children will challenge themselves and be less afraid, but don't push your children with your own goals in mind. If you change your thinking to be less fearful, more accepting, and open to new ideas, you will help your children produce more in their lives. They will emulate you and want to try more things, and confidently and critically develop their own ideas, just as you have shown them.

Learn to see the glass as half full, and be positive because life is hard and life goes on and we need to think positively or we go under. We want to teach our kids to swim in this sea of life with all its gifts, good and bad. There is always a lesson, always a chance to grow.

Teach kids about differences in a positive way that doesn't exploit people or put them down. Think about your values, and what you want your child to learn. If your main objective is to teach your kid to be tough, get rich, or to be a better sports player than any of his friends, then you might learn how to sponsor other desired things in your child after reading this book. Let your goal as a parent be to create a child who is kinder, more empathic, open minded, self confident, and able to manage emotions and thinking. Give your child the opportunity to think about others, and how life events affect them. Let them know how you or someone else handled a challenging situation. We are always striving to teach emotional awareness. Teach your child to have humility, to admit mistakes, learn from them and move on. Create a child who makes the world a kinder place, a child who cares about others, values people and life, expresses feelings openly with awareness, and can be a team player, Teach your children well, and they will have friends, find valuable work, and truly direct their own lives.

RESPECT YOUR CHILD'S FEELINGS

Hold family meetings where all are afforded a chance to speak their concerns, joys and feelings in a safe family atmosphere. Speak your mind when you feel you are taken for granted or treated unfairly by your kids or other family members. Foster your child's interests and feelings without control, with love.

Most of all, listen to what kids tell you they need.

I recently was deciding whether to send my son to full-time or half-time hockey camp, so I asked him what he'd like. He said it was summer and he didn't want to dress up in hot hockey clothes and be indoors all day. He'd prefer to do hockey in the fall and spend summer days outside. I respected this.

Just remember, if you sponsor children's abilities to know their feelings, value their feelings and let them speak up for themselves, and having their views acknowledged, they will learn to be healthy adults who know their needs.

Think of the skills an adult has when they can know a job doesn't satisfy them and move on, or can ask for a raise confidently. Many adults stay stuck because they never learned to get their needs met.

We are only on this planet for a short while. Laugh, live freely, speak freely, flow, flow, flow.

TWELVE

Closing Thoughts

A MORTAL CHALLENGE

Never was I challenged to put into practice what I learned about emotional development and had always taught my children, until in July, 2000, my husband was diagnosed with advanced colon cancer and given three months to live. All of my intellectual abilities went out the window as I watched him struggle to live for one year, sick and on tremendous doses of pills and chemotherapy. Our lives were all put on hold, and we knew that he would die, it was just a question of when. My children faced the biggest challenge of all time — watching someone you love die in front of you day by day. The open communication of feelings and what was happening to my family saved my children. If

I hadn't been able to talk freely to them, there would have been no outlet for their grief, fear, anger, pain, and all the emotions surrounding loss, in the face of death. I believe their ability to handle this situation would have been compromised if I hadn't been able to use positive thinking consciously, even though — believe me — I didn't always feel that way.

During this challenging year, friends, family and sometimes acquaintances would share with me deaths of loved ones and many would mention the secrecy in the family, the inability to express feelings related to the death, and how this negatively impacted them. My children, because of my awareness of this need, were informed that their dad could die, and we spent many nights dealing with their feelings and questions about this. Sometimes they were furious because their Dad wasn't there or available to them. I'd always talk to them about this, and let them express those feelings openly. Nothing was hidden or secretive. We were faced with challenging life questions, such as: Why does this happen to people at such a young age? Why their dad? Why didn't God help him? Would they die too? These questions all relate to the uncertainty of life that all of us are confronted with at some time or another. Only my kids had to face this early on. But talking about this opened them to the understanding that it's not what happens in life, it's how you deal with it. This is a very important lesson, probably the most important, one ever has to learn, child or adult.

THE NEED FOR FAITH

Faith, another word for positive thinking and another form of emotional development, got us through. Our faith was believing that we could handle this situation. We knew that we would be sad, but we also thought about everyone who helped us and cared for us, and how lucky we were. We never went unaware of what was there for us. The world was very safe to my children, by the availability, kindness and hope showed by others. We had faith in us, a power greater than us, and in people because through experiences like ours, one realizes that there are some things much too hard to handle in life alone with our limited capabilities. People need others and support. People need hope that they will be ok, can trust in their own power and a higher power based on their own belief system. A higher power/God can be whatever you believe. The traditional God for many. Nature and the power of love amongst people can be someone else's higher power. Whatever works is what counts. It's important for children to have faith in the power of the universe, a power greater than them, and to have faith that people and the universe and their higher power will be there to call on in need. My children acquired that faith; we didn't go to church and weren't following a specific religious doctrine. They relied on their emotional world, a belief and intuitive feeling that Dad's spirit would always be with them and could never die. They felt it, they looked for it, they held onto it, and still do.

The spirit of their dad is their emotional development in action. The physical world is tangible, visible, and based on empirical evidence. The spiritual world is based on trust, intuition, faith, hope, love — all the emotional feelings that we want to promote when we speak of emotional development.

SEPTEMBER 11

When we view our world today, we see how emotional development is lacking everywhere, and we see it blossoming everywhere. When I am in yoga class, bowing to and respecting other people, I am very far away from the anger and lack of emotional and spiritual connection we saw on September 11th, 2001. Throughout time, in wars across the globe, we have seen people and countries lacking respect for each other and wanting to be right. In order to make this world a better, more loving and peaceful place to be, we must sponsor love, emotional connection, peace, and understanding of differences in our children.

September 11th was a perfect time to teach them about the lack of emotional development in our world. Unfortunately, many lacking in emotional and psychological awareness explained this as an act of the "bad guys" hurting the "good guys." The message to the children needs to be about sponsoring more understanding, love, lack of hate, less self-righteousness, and more compassion in our world. We have the problems in this world because we are human and haven't risen to this advanced emotional state. We can try to get there, little by little, by all doing our part to promote emotional awareness and healthy thinking. We can see the task at hand.

But the task at hand is a positive challenge. Imagine working toward creating a child that thinks, feels comfortable in his/her own skin, and is accepting of his/her ideas and others. Imagine working toward creating a child who is open minded, and confident to make changes in her/his self and the world. In years to come the world can be a better place with an emotionally aware group of inhabitants. This might sound like a science fiction movie to you. That's what is so wonderful about science fiction as a means of communicating a well needed message. Still, it is possible to work toward this goal. Every ounce of progress counts.

Be confident to promote emotional awareness and development in your children. Enjoy the confidence and self awareness this job will offer you as the parents. Remember, "Change your thoughts and change your life experiences." Talk openly with your children, promoting the expression of their ideas and feelings. They will learn to live in this world physically, but to rely on their inner world, their higher self as their guide. You will offer them the greatest gift of all — self-reliance, confidence, understanding, forgiveness, and self-love.

"Life isn't about finding yourself.
Life is about creating yourself."

Unknown

About the Author

Sally Sacks is a licensed marriage and family counselor in private practice in Westford, Massachussetts. She specializes in teaching clients to communicate effectively in order to help them achieve what they want from themselves and in their relationships with others. She believes that thinking effectively is an art that not everyone is born with but which it is possible for everyone to learn, and she has taught hundreds of people how to challenge their thinking. She has taught classes on how to refocus and retrain thinking in schools, hospitals, and mental health clinics, and she helped found two counseling centers with a specfic focus on the mind/body connection. She lives with her partner, Charles, and their three children.

For copies of Sally's book, *How To Raise The Next President,* please contact her at *sally.sacks@verizon.net.*